Praise for *Rebooting Work*

"People do not like to be managed, but they love to be led. *Rebooting Work* introduces a new vision for work, and Maynard Webb leads readers to a place they want to go, one that has less traffic congestion and a better work-life balance."

> —**Scott McNealy**, cofounder, Sun Microsystems; chairman, Wayin; founder, Curriki

"In every corner of society, there are optimists, agitators, and rabble-rousers—people who have never lost hope that it is possible to create change. Maynard Webb has created economic and technological change through so many companies he's helped build. In *Rebooting Work*, he takes his message of hope to change how the world works."

> —**Jeffrey Skoll**, founder and chairman, Participant Media; founder and chairman, the Skoll Foundation; former president, eBay

"As you go and pursue career goals, it's important to do something that you love. *Rebooting Work* acknowledges the importance of putting passion and purpose in work. Maynard Webb—Silicon Valley's go-to guy to get stuff done—gives you a framework to help you get there."

> —**Jeffrey Housenbold**, president and CEO, Shutterfly

"*Rebooting Work* is as profound as it is a pleasure to read. Not only will this book help you achieve the happiness that comes with being fulfilled, it will also help companies achieve far more by cultivating and supporting motivated and high-spirited people."

> —**James M. Citrin**, leader, CEO, and board practice, Spencer Stuart; author, *You Need a Leader, Now What?*

"The social and mobile revolution is forcing customer service contact centers to go social or get left behind with decreased customer loyalty and loss of market share. We're seeing companies transform their businesses and reach new heights of success by integrating social and mobile capabilities in their customer service contact center. *Rebooting Work* takes a different angle on the revolution—how this positively impacts individuals—and shows anyone how to get on board."

> —**Marty Beard**, president and CEO, LiveOps

"We are all entrepreneurs, accountable for our own professional destiny—whether we are launching a technology startup or working in a large corporation. This unique and accessible book is one big Silicon Valley mentoring session, delivered by a battle-tested executive with a can-do attitude."

> —**Thomas J. Tierney**, cofounder and chairman, Bridgespan Group; former CEO, Bain & Company; coauthor, *Aligning the Stars* and *Give Smart*

"Maynard Webb understands the importance of thinking big and starting small. *Rebooting Work* is an engaging and informative book that helps readers find clarity of purpose. It will influence entrepreneurs for years to come."

> —**Jim Goetz**, general partner, Sequoia Capital

"Enlightening, entertaining, extremely practical. Maynard Webb has given us the best kind of business book: a treasure-trove of practical wisdom woven into a fascinating story. If you are looking for a highly readable map to business success in the 21st century, look no further. Maynard Webb helped invent the new technological world we live in, and no one knows better how to channel the power of technology while maintaining the essential heart-connections that allow work to be a source of joy and life-satisfaction. Get this book! Reading *Rebooting Work* could well be the best investment you make this year."

> —**Gay Hendricks**, author, *The Big Leap* and *The Corporate Mystic*

"Seeing trends in technology early is what matters. Maynard Webb sees them early, and *Rebooting Work* covers what's next in IT and how to use it to transform work and your life."

> —**Matt Carey**, executive VP and CIO, the Home Depot

"A near perfect storm of digital technologies has enabled the emergence of electronic marketplaces for everything from stocks to antiques. In *Rebooting Work*, Maynard Webb compellingly illustrates the emergent electronic marketplace for jobs and the profound implications this has for our careers."

> —**William A. Thornton**, former CTO, Fidelity Investments

Rebooting WORK

Transform How You Work in the AGE OF ENTREPRENEURSHIP

Maynard Webb
and Carlye Adler

JOSSEY-BASS
A Wiley Imprint
www.josseybass.com

Published by Jossey-Bass
A Wiley Imprint
One Montgomery Street, Suite 1200, San Francisco, CA 94104-4594
www.josseybass.com

Cover image copyright: Ilin Sergey
Cover design: Adrian Morgan

Jossey-Bass books and products are available through most bookstores. To contact Jossey-Bass directly call our Customer Care Department within the U.S. at 800-956-7739, outside the U.S. at 317-572-3986, or fax 317-572-4002.

Wiley publishes in a variety of print and electronic formats and by print-on-demand. Some material included with standard print versions of this book may not be included in e-books or in print-on-demand. If this book refers to media such as a CD or DVD that is not included in the version you purchased, you may download this material at **http://booksupport.wiley.com**. For more information about Wiley products, visit **www.wiley.com**.

Library of Congress Cataloging-in-Publication Data
Webb, Maynard, 1955–
    Rebooting work : transform how you work in the age of entrepreneurship / Maynard Webb and Carlye Adler.—1st ed.
        p. cm.
    Includes bibliographical references and index.
    ISBN 978-1-118-22615-5 (cloth); ISBN 978-1-118-41952-6 (ebk);
ISBN 978-1-118-42124-6 (ebk); ISBN 978-1-118-43387-4 (ebk)
    1. Career development. 2. Job satisfaction 3. Change (Psychology) 4. Organizational change. 5. Personnel management. I. Adler, Carlye. II. Title.
    HF5381.W39 2013
    650.1 —dc23
                                                                2012037635

Printed in the United States of America
FIRST EDITION
HB Printing   10 9 8 7 6 5 4 3 2 1

To my coaches,
who inspired and brought out the best in me,
and to the teams that I was privileged to be a part of

Contents

Part 3   Getting Started

Foreword:
The Benchmark of Success

By Meg Whitman

There are people you encounter in life who stand out above all others—who teach you, challenge you, and inspire you. In my life, one of those people has been Maynard Webb.

I first met Maynard in 1999, shortly after I became the CEO of eBay. The company was growing very quickly, and it was an incredibly exciting time. But one of the challenges we had to contend with was the stability of the site. Our technology, built when we were a fledgling start-up, just couldn't keep up with the growing transaction volumes. The site was frequently breaking down and disappointing sellers and buyers in the process. One particularly severe outage lasted for twenty-two hours. It attracted enormous national news media attention and nearly cost us all of our customer data.

The outages required me to look for someone strong and smart enough to tackle the problems. We simply didn't have the in-house talent to fix the site. We needed someone to come in and rapidly overhaul the technology while we continued to grow and do business. I described it as changing an airplane's engines in flight without losing altitude or crashing.

As I started my search for a great technologist, I began to hear about Maynard Webb. Maynard was the widely respected chief information officer (CIO) at PC maker Gateway and had previously been at Bay Networks, where he completed a notoriously challenging SAP implementation in a remarkable nine months. This sounded like the guy we needed, but unfortunately for eBay, Maynard wasn't looking for a new job.

After some prodding from our recruiter, Maynard agreed to meet with me in California. True to his nature, Maynard thought the challenges eBay faced were "awesome." eBay was just the kind of job Maynard loved—a big, hairy problem no one else wanted, but that if solved, would make a huge impact.

About a week after our meeting, Maynard agreed to join eBay. For the next seven years, Maynard solved every problem we threw at him. Maynard rebuilt our technology infrastructure and took what was once a big liability and turned it into an area of strategic strength. Over time, he built a world-class technology team that has, as he likes to say, been "breaking new snow" ever since.

And what Maynard's team created was awe inspiring. The new ultrareliable infrastructure they engineered and the quality measures they put in place helped sustain the company's explosive growth. It enabled the site to scale to handle more than a billion transactions per day and store over two petabytes of data—two hundred times more data than contained in the Library of Congress.

Maynard architected much more than eBay's technology, though. Later, as eBay's COO, Maynard helped introduce the processes and day-to-day operating structures that moved us from a business of 250 employees to a global company of more than 10,000 employees. In his seven-year tenure, Maynard enabled eBay to effectively grow revenue from $140 million to more than $5 billion by the time he left in mid-2006.

In working so closely with Maynard for so long, I noticed how much he enjoyed being a mentor. He always made time for anyone who wanted his advice—and there are many who sought him out. He hosted regular "fireside chats" in eBay's offices, in which he shared his career experiences and insights with intimate groups of twenty people; they became very popular and allowed him to reach more employees.

At one of our annual Leaders' Meetings, Maynard told a story I will never forget. He spoke about sitting on a park bench long after he retired. He was no longer the boss, had no budget, and could no longer hand out a job or a promotion. There was no ulterior motive to be nice to him. Maynard wondered if the people he encountered throughout his life would walk over to say hello or turn and walk away. He then stressed the value of conducting oneself in ways that draw people toward you.

When Maynard left eBay, we dedicated the park benches in our new courtyard to him. We inscribed a quote from Maynard on each one, a piece of wisdom from him that continues to guide us. And when Maynard comes back to visit and sits on one of his benches, I know no one will ever walk by without stopping to say hello.

Though I was sad when Maynard left eBay, I also understood. He had finished what he had come to do. It was time for new challenges.

As CEO of LiveOps, Maynard helped a new generation of workers prosper on their own terms. He also started investing in innovative companies that are leveraging technology to help workers find greater levels of achievement and personal fulfillment. Maynard serves on the boards of salesforce.com and Yahoo!, companies he believes embody his focus on people, success, and a better future.

Rebooting Work takes on a big problem—the broken state of work—and reveals a solution, one that is better for employees and employers. As with every problem Maynard solves, he has ferreted out the answers and made certain that his solutions are easy to understand and possible to implement.

This book is the result of Maynard's journey through an exciting and varied career. It makes Maynard's knowledge and mentorship accessible to everyone. It will help people become the "CEOs of their own destiny" and live happier and more fulfilling lives. And it will help companies operate better as they move forward into the evolving landscape of work in the twenty-first century.

Preface

As the chairman of a cloud computing company that creates work opportunities for thousands of people (contractors and employees) each month, I see the world of work as very different from the one that's being reported in the headlines. I'm convinced that this is one of the most exciting times in the history of work—and one of the best times for anyone to enter the workforce. Just as the Industrial Revolution was defined by manufacturing that gave people jobs, today's IT revolution—defined by new technologies—is giving people more flexible and empowering opportunities for work than ever before.

When I started working, I had to leave my home in Florida and take a permanent job with IBM in Minnesota. I've moved nine times for a job, and I moved three times in less than two years. We all know that this model is steeped in the past, but two years ago, as I started to think about what was happening in the world of work—and about writing this book—I realized that even though those IBM days were long behind me, there were other outdated work models that I was perpetuating and that were not right for me or my family. My career was still defined by the limits of working for a company. I was working with assigned teams that were static, and we worked from the same location. I spent set hours in an office building and not enough time with my wife and family.

Once I became involved with LiveOps and became inspired by the twenty thousand independent agents who were truly working on their own, I realized that there was a better model for working. They were paid for performance, but they worked on their own terms and were happy with their freedom. It was great for them and great for our company. It was a win-win for workers and management like nothing I had experienced before. I bought into it so much that I decided that I needed to walk the talk myself. I gave up formal operating roles and began to reframe the way I thought about my career.

In many ways, I've been very blessed—I am married to the love of my life; I have wonderful children and grandchildren. I've enjoyed a career in technology that has inspired me and provided for my family beyond my wildest imagination. I've also had some body blows. The times I've been thrown a curve ball or knocked down have been just as influential—perhaps more influential—in determining the ultimate outcome of my life.

Over my career, I have had the good fortune of being in the right place at the right time in several industries. I was thus able to witness and participate in significant transformations in technology, which gave me good strategic insights into where the world was going. I worked at IBM during the PC revolution, focusing on computer security long before it was "cool" or even possible to be a hacker. During the PC heyday, I was transferred to Boca Raton and put in charge of financial systems integrity, which at the time was in a shambles. I worked at Thomas-Conrad as "networking" began taking off, and at Bay Networks as the Internet exploded. I was at the epicenter of Internet commerce at eBay and in the middle of the revolution in work at LiveOps. My extracurricular activities as a board member at Gartner and at visionary companies including salesforce.com and AdMob allowed me to see such technology trends as cloud computing and mobile long before they were hot.

With the insight that comes from hindsight, I now realize that the most interesting parts of my career happened when there was something that urgently needed fixing, and it was also in an area of nascent strategic importance. I was never interested in just doing something that anyone could do; I was always fascinated by aiming high—shooting for something that would be truly marvelous.

As lucky as my story is, it is also in many ways an unlikely one. I grew up in West Palm Beach, Florida, the third of five kids, and my family was considered upper-middle class. My father was a real estate appraiser and the president of his own company. My mother was a stay-at-home mom who took care of the kids and my father's mother, who lived with us. Life was good: playing outdoors, figuring out ways to finagle out of piano lessons. Then, everything changed dramatically when my father died suddenly from a stroke ten days before my seventh birthday.

My father held no life insurance, and our small savings account quickly ran out. Growing up with little money, we learned to make sacrifices. For several months, we lived without hot water. For a couple of years, we lived without a TV. I couldn't join the Cub Scouts because it required my mom to serve as a den mother, which she didn't have time to do because she was working. Of course, the biggest loss was not getting to live with—or really know—my father.

My mom had a college education and went back to teaching to support the family, first as a boys' physical education teacher, the only opening at the time, then as a science teacher. Two years after my dad died, she decided to pursue her master's degree so that she could make more money. I was nine at the time. That summer, Mom enrolled at San Jose State in California, and with her five children moved into the dorms. There, our after-school fun involved learning to play poker from the other grad students. My mom was incredibly strong, and also industrious. After that summer in California, we moved back to Florida, where she would eventually run the Jupiter Marine Science Center and was voted Teacher of the Year for the State of Florida, one of many accolades she would receive. I had so much love and admiration for her, but was troubled by the position in which my father had left us.

I promised myself then that when I had kids, I would not leave them unprotected as we had been. I also became convinced that I would die at a young age, as my father had. That drove me; I expected life to be short, so I needed to get going at achieving all that I wanted.

I always wanted to work, and when I was ten, I secured a route selling TV guides. (It was small; I had three customers.) By the time I was twelve, I took on a paper route. My mom would wake me before dawn to get to the local gas station and fold the papers before delivering them. I was so exhausted by the end of the day that I'd fall asleep on the floor of the living room.

The thing I loved the most about being a paperboy was the tips I earned around Christmas. One year, I used these funds to buy a Ping-Pong table for my family. I worked several jobs over the next several years: at a gas station, cleaning toilets at

Mister Donut, busing tables at the Pancake House, working at an outdoor store, and doing the night shift at a mattress factory.

These were small jobs, but I dreamed big. As a kid, that meant a career as a Major League Baseball player. When I was nine, I was told I shouldn't try out for Little League, as the rest of the new kids were ten. I wanted to anyway. I had my brother's hand-me-down glove, and because he was left-handed, I struggled to catch well as a righty, but I practiced relentlessly and ultimately made the team. I played sports throughout school; our Babe Ruth All-Star team even won a state championship. My athletic career culminated in being recruited for football to the U.S. Naval Academy in Annapolis.

That was 1974, and I had grown long hair and decided I didn't want to go to Annapolis. My mom was very disappointed, as my dad had been a naval officer, and she felt that I was throwing away an opportunity for a great (and paid for) education. I found myself on a different path, though. I went to college in Florida and studied criminal justice. I worked throughout school, even creating a retail business at a local wholesale nursery, and I interned at IBM during my senior year.

Upon graduation, I was offered a full-time job as an entry-level security guard at IBM in Minnesota. Considering my thirty-five-year career in the technology industry, some people assume I mean computer security, but at the time, computer security was in its infancy. (It was a mainframe and minicomputer world.) I worked in physical security, protecting the buildings and its employees.

Every day brought something different. I worked in the lobby of the office building. I also toured through the halls, ensuring that the building was safe and that people got to where they needed to go. No job was too small or too big. I took the flag down at night, assisted with first aid, and one time had to handle a situation where an employee murdered his wife and then killed himself.

Within a year, I was offered a chance to move to a new facility in North Carolina, and shortly thereafter was promoted to become a supervisor of security guards. The physical security work segued into product security—I was in charge of securely administering the most confidential documents at our location and also checking up on how our vendors secured our information.

Then, within five years, as technology evolved, I moved into computer security. Both computer and physical security were becoming hot topics, as we had experienced attacks on our physical premises and had concerns about computer espionage. Although I transitioned from blue collar to white collar, I never gave up my blue-collar approach to work. I continued to understand the value of heavy lifting, and perhaps my willingness to do heavy lifting became my greatest strength.

Breaking Systems

I love new technology, and I'm obsessed with how it makes our lives better, but my role in the technology industry has never been that of the dreamer. I've always been the doer. I've been fortunate enough to work for companies that allowed me to witness the birth of new groundbreaking technologies, but in every company in which I worked, I was brought in because there was a difficulty on the path to growth or advancement. In each job there was a problem, a big issue that seemed insurmountable. While others seemed turned off by these types of challenges, I was really excited by the opportunity to fix something—the chance to make a difference.

Sometimes my job also meant that in trying to fix something, I had to figure out how to break it. At IBM, one of my early jobs in computer security was indeed breaking systems. That was a very cool job. I would be sent to a location, given general access to the systems, and told, "See what you can do." With that mandate, I was able to confiscate highly confidential documents, take over operating systems, and once even cut a check for a significant amount of money. (I returned it.) It was fun breaking systems, and it gave me insight into how to fix them. Determining what is wrong with something and trying to find a solution has been the thread that has tied my career together.

The truth is, I was unqualified for many of my career roles when I was assigned to them. However, no one else was willing to do them, so I volunteered. Some people called me insane, but in every opportunity that I signed up for, I was very confident that I could do the job well, and tackled the challenges with gusto and no fear. Several times this led to approaches that weren't considered normal practice, but to me they made common sense, and I've always allowed common sense to lead.

For example, when I was doing product security at IBM, vendor security was taken very seriously—vendors were required to log visitors, physically lock documents, and track the removal of files. Amazingly, though, no one thought to lock up the files on the computers. There was no security system in place to protect the digital versions. That was a big gap. The product and security guys had to learn to become more computer literate, and I helped lead that charge. At first this idea was seen as unconventional, but soon, as everything went digital, it became an everyday imperative.

Later, when I was working as a network director at Quantum, a disk drive manufacturer, we had a pressing deadline to get long-distance circuits and technology infrastructure into new factories that were coming on line. Not one telecom vendor said it could meet this deadline. This was not a good outcome; it would delay everything, thus costing us a considerable amount of money. I called a meeting with all the vendor representatives together to address the situation. I explained that the suppliers who were willing to find a way to work with us would build a long and profitable partnership with our company. I then challenged them to find a way to help us. All it took was for one rep to raise his hand and say he could do it. The others followed, all committing to find a way to make an exception. We delivered the project on time.

I went from Quantum to Bay Networks as CIO. The CIO role was very new and was just beginning to be elevated to the executive table. It is actually the only job in my career that I have done multiple times. It is very strategic, very hard, and very risky; at the time, most people said CIO stood for "Career Is Over." I loved the role and the challenges that came with it.

At Bay Networks we faced very serious issues. We were merging two companies, SynOptics and Wellfleet, onto a common architecture and platform. I agreed to do an aggressive enterprise resource planning (ERP) implementation worldwide, which had been tried several times before and met with failure. I committed to do the implementation in twelve months, and the first step was to ensure that everyone was playing on the same team. I created a mandate that enforced timely decisions (within twenty-four hours) and key executive involvement. I created an untraditional bonus structure that was collaborative with our vendors. For example, our consultants at Accenture were on the same bonus plan as our executive stakeholders, which created a win-win environment. Nobody could go home on Friday unless the week's open issues were rectified. And there were consequences: one factory wouldn't go fast enough, so we pulled it out of the scope. We completed the effort in nine months—at the time it was one of the fastest ERP implementations in the world. We even received a Computerworld Smithsonian IT nomination for the project.

I left Bay Networks after about four years to join Gateway Computers, which was facing many growth challenges. I was hired to significantly improve its web capability, but was surprised to learn upon arrival that although the year 2000 was only two years away, the company was not Y2K ready on its legacy systems. I led a major project to address that, as well as developed a radically different systems architecture.

In 1999, I was heavily recruited by eBay to become its president of technology. The company had some very sizeable technology issues, including one twenty-two-hour outage of its whole service. It was a very public debacle, and unfortunately the site had become the poster child for instability. I found that a crucial part of the solution involved taking a collaborative approach. I encouraged our partners to work with us in a way that they had not in the past. For example, we were using Sun servers, and as a way to motivate our vendor to be a real partner, I suggested that it carry our availability as a metric for executives' bonus plans. This had never been done before, but it worked for both parties, and later Sun adopted this model with its top customers.

The team was fabulous; we worked extremely hard and turned things around. We were growing so fast that we outgrew being able to use one big back-end database server to run our site. We either had to transition to a mainframe system or implement a dramatically different approach. We chose to implement a distributed architecture (what we called a small soldiers approach), which enabled us to achieve scale and stability much more quickly by distributing the database traffic across many different servers as opposed to one. We became world class at innovating on time and at a high velocity without impacting site availability. It was at the time unprecedented to be able to fix the site and keep it running while simultaneously adding new features, functions, and capabilities.

I stayed at eBay for seven years, the last four as chief operating officer. As COO, I helped codify and establish the company's culture, implement decision-making models, and oversee the budget process and corporate initiatives, along with managing all my functional areas (trust and safety, customer support, HR, billing, technology, and product management). I was charged with managing executive staff and helping to administrate the board. I did the same thing for the company that I had done for the technology: implement processes that would ensure that it could scale while facing hyper growth.

Early on in my career, a very seasoned technology veteran at IBM once told me, "What's beautiful about working with you, Maynard, is you haven't been trained on why this is impossible."

It's true: my training happened on the job, so I didn't know what was deemed unprecedented or insurmountable. I'm grateful for the fresh perspective that inexperience provided; it not only gave me the confidence that I could get the job done but also afforded the most interesting and most rewarding opportunities. I began to become recognized for my willingness to do the jobs no one wanted, and top technology leaders began to rely on me to solve daunting problems. That's how I became known by some as Mr. Fix-It.

———————

Although this book is not my memoir, in some instances my personal experiences can help illustrate some of the big ideas here—on how we can transform the way we work in a shifting global workforce. The one thing my career has taught me is that instead of fearing change, you must be willing to embrace it is key. With this attitude, in addition to a passion for understanding technological breakthroughs, you can often be the first to new markets and new opportunities.

In addition to using examples from companies where I have worked and companies of which I am a board member, I will mention companies I have invested in, as those are the ones I know the most about and can give detailed examples for.

If I did it—an underdog with a humble beginning and no special connections, raised by a single mother with five kids; someone who didn't go to the best schools, get an engineering degree, or earn a master's degree; someone who started his career as a security guard and never had the "executive look"—then, without a doubt, you can do it too. Sometimes it just takes the right attitude and the confidence to know that the old way isn't necessarily the right way—and the belief that better days are always ahead.

November 2012

Maynard Webb
Silicon Valley

Introduction

In my last corporate job, as the CEO of cloud-based call center LiveOps, I was hired to scale a start-up company to become a mature, fast-growing, operationally excellent technology company, but something else unexpected happened. I began to see how big of a problem work has become for most of us, and how much we could change to make it better. I learned about how many people were unhappy and unfulfilled and was eager for an alternative way that would give them more control over their lives.

This dissatisfaction was widespread—and alarming. One survey found that less than half of Americans (just 47 percent) are satisfied with their work.[1] (When the Conference Board's first survey was conducted in 1987, most workers—61 percent—said they were happy in their job.)

As an employer, I know that this decline in job satisfaction is unacceptable and dangerous. Another survey by consulting firm Mercer found that the most discontented are young employees; 44 percent of those ages sixteen to twenty-four and 40 percent of the twenty-five- to thirty-four-year-olds say they "seriously are considering leaving" their jobs.[2]

That too is a big problem. Working adults spend more of their waking hours at work than anywhere else. Work should be a place of inspiration and innovation; it should not—it cannot—be unfulfilling. But for all too many, it is. The degree to which work adversely affects our lives, and how much we come to regret it later, is disconcerting. Bronnie Ware, an Australian palliative care nurse, who worked with patients in the last twelve weeks of their lives, shared their thoughts in a blog called *Inspiration and Chai*, which she later turned into a book called *The Top Five Regrets of the Dying*. She found common themes in what people regretted and what we could learn from them. The top two lessons: "I wish I'd had the courage to live a life true to myself, not the life others expected of me," and "I wish I hadn't worked so hard."[3] When people realize that their life is almost over and look back on it, they see how many dreams have gone unfulfilled. Most people had not honored even a half of their dreams due to choices they had or had not made.

That's upsetting, but what gets me most agitated is that it does not have to be this way. The things that people don't like about work—toiling away so many hours in office buildings, spending too much time in cars commuting to work, and ceding control to a company—no longer have to be facts of work life. Technology has evolved to the point that many of our practices and methods around work could change radically. Advances in cloud services, Internet telephony, wireless technology, and mobile computing can be applied to change work and make it better pretty quickly, and pretty easily. Social technologies, which enable us to know exactly what our long-lost friends are doing in their spare time, can help us better understand what is happening in our businesses. As an investor in start-up companies and someone who meets young, gifted entrepreneurs who dream about the future every day, I gain insight and access into other new technologies that can help us revolutionize work even further. There are so many new services and apps and ideas that make work easier, more engaging, and more rewarding. There are so many ways to take out the pain points and allow the soul food to be put back in.

Although technology is a path to a better and brighter future, it is only an enabler. After all, *technology* is a word that describes the concepts, techniques, and methods having to do with how to accomplish a task. Before we implement methods and plans and action items, though, we need to take a step back. We need to change the way we think about work. If we want to change it, we need to look back and study how we got here, then determine how we can forge ahead.

I wrote this book to investigate how the current work crisis came about, and to help individuals understand that it is within their power to end it and move on to careers that can provide both fulfillment and financial security. In addition to advocating for the personal joy that comes with being fulfilled, I also come at this with the perspective of an executive and manager and strongly believe that companies achieve far more with motivated and happy people.

Rebooting Work explores the emerging technologies and techniques that can enable every individual to make this shift to take charge of his or her own career. It's not just a better way—it's essential for the new era we live in, which is defined by an entrepreneurial spirit. The old ways of working, which may have led previous generations to success, no longer guarantee the same results. We are seeing new trends increasingly change work. Online freelance job postings have skyrocketed over the last few years, and companies increasingly outsource work. The shift under way to an information economy is as important as the last great shift, when we transitioned from an agricultural to an industrial economy nearly one hundred years ago.[4]

MERITOCRACY VERSUS ENTITLEMENT AND THE AGE OF ENTREPRENEURSHIP

Each year more than 1.1 million American high school students play football. The best of them, the star quarterbacks, running backs, linebackers, and linemen, dream of scoring scholarships to play college ball, but only twenty thousand—just 6 percent of seniors on the team—will play their freshman year of college. By their final year, that number dwindles to fifteen thousand athletes. Only 255 of those elite players are drafted to the NFL. The chance of making it to the pros if you play in high school? A very small number: a mere 0.08 percent.[5]

And if you think that once players make it to the pros they can take a rest, think again. Every player in the NFL must get revoted on to the team every year. No one can buy his way on to the team. It's a model of ruthless efficiency that ensures that every player brings his A-game every time he steps onto the field. It's a system that makes football an incredible game to watch.

I've always been inspired by sports, and throughout my career have taken the lessons I learned playing football and baseball growing up, as well as what I've witnessed through following professional sports, into the work world. Team dynamics and the importance of learning to win—and lose—gracefully were invaluable lessons to me in building my career. Further, the need to get voted on to the team every day inspired me to demand the most from myself and my teams. I have found that being transparent about performance—a tactic learned from studying baseball stats—let people know where they stood and inspired a continuous quest for improvement.

What I'm talking about is meritocracy: a system that rewards individuals based on performance and results. It's an idea that carries weight for employees in the workplace. There also are benefits for companies that operate on this principle by committing to being open and transparent about their performance. (For example, a website should publish real-time information about its availability and system performance time, as eBay does with its announcement board or as salesforce.com does with its Trust Site.)

But what I've also found is that although we have some great examples of companies that are transparent about their performance, overall, most corporations don't follow these tenets when it comes to how they evaluate or treat their employees. In fact, traditional company culture is quite the opposite of a performance-based meritocracy. Historically—meaning in the past fifty or so years—loyalty was given higher priority than achievements and results. Outside of sales organizations, goals, and ways to measure goals, were not always clear. How an individual was performing and how she stacked up against others were not often transparent.

Although one would expect the rules of the ball park to be different from the rules of the office park, I found that by ignoring what made sports so great—essentially its functioning as a meritocracy—we were missing out on an opportunity to make work *work* better. The desire for security trumped the drive to be spectacular. Everyone played it too safe. And this has stymied both employees and employers.

How come as a society we support a model that embraces meritocracy—in which the best athletes, those with the best skills, are known and rise to the top—but we don't demand a similar model at work? Generally speaking, we accept this system in school, where grades are based on performance against one's peers, not just on showing up to class. How is it that at work we fear systems that allow us to see how we are doing compared to others, that motivate us to do better work every day, and that reward us for our meaningful contributions instead of our blind commitment? Why are both employees and employers so afraid of operating in a meritocracy, which rewards them for how well they perform, not for how long they've been performing?

At work, both employees and employers often fall into an entitlement mentality. For example, some employers do everything they can to keep the talent inside their walls hidden from everyone else, lest they be "poached." They feel as though they know what is best for the employee and must make sure that the employee knows how to be successful in their company. Employees who leave are often shunned as being disloyal. For employees, there's an expectation that they will be given a job, and as long as they are doing okay, they expect to keep it. By keeping their head down, doing a mediocre job, and not being a problem, they believe they will be rewarded.

I have always been amazed by how managers seldom actually want to have truthful discussions about how someone is performing, even when that individual is doing great. As a manager, I have often implemented informal weekly and formal quarterly check-ins in an effort to force a dialogue and prevent a big disconnect at the end of the year for many employees, when they find out they were not doing as well as their perception led them to believe. Think of all the wasted time and productivity when we give performance feedback only on a yearly basis. The world doesn't operate on this type of clock anymore. When everything is happening in real time, even my formal quarterly meetings seem grossly inadequate. As a board member of a well-known technology company, I witnessed a once well-respected CEO lose the trust of his board and employees in less than ten days. In the current business environment, the idea of an annual review is so antiquated, it's comical. We live in a world in which countries have been toppled in months, or even days, but certainly not years. It's a world in which much is decided instantaneously, and the workplace must adapt.

Yet we are very far from this kind of culture. How can work be so out of touch with the way the rest of the world is headed?

I'm a strong proponent of meritocracy, of the value of hard work over entitlement, of talent over tenure, and of transparency over closed systems, probably because of where I came from—and because of where I am today. I believe that many executives hold these beliefs. I have gained significant freedom by embracing a mind-set of meritocracy. I've seen what it can inspire, unlock, and unleash, and I've also seen how the opposite—an organization that supports entitlement over results—can limit growth and opportunity.

Unlike the past when you got news and information from only one or two sources and a couple of times a day, today you get information in real time and from multiple sources. There is no place to hide. You can hope to keep problems in-house, but you're unlikely to succeed. Problems do not get better with time; they get far worse. They spin out of control faster today than ever before. The only way to deal with this is to be open and transparent. If you have a problem, admit it, apologize, and fix it. No one expects perfection, but they do expect honesty. Now, meritocracy over entitlement is the only way. We are in a new age—one that is more transparent thanks to the Internet and one that is being defined by a new generation of workers who grew up with more technology and a more entrepreneurial mind-set.

––––––––––––

My background is really in operations. I see systems not working, I am called in when they are failing, and I must determine how to fix them. Whether it's an e-commerce start-up with an unreliable website, a public company trying to implement a new systems architecture, or a legacy company trying to carve a path for the future with new leadership, I find that by asking the right questions, you can get to the root of the problem and come up with a solution. With work it's no different, and I have created a model, a framework, to impart everything you need to know about how to operate in a new world of work. This model, which we'll explore in detail in Part Two, is designed to help individuals become accountable for their own success. With that accountability comes a new and refreshing freedom—it puts you back in charge of your life, shifting control from your boss to yourself. Essentially, it allows you to become the CEO of your own destiny and to be the one in charge of your career—and your life.

The framework in this book is the culmination of years of experience in managing and mentoring, and, I hope, will serve as a template for you as you begin to rework how you think about work. It identifies four different philosophies around work: Company Man or Woman, CEO of Your Own Destiny, Disenchanted Employee, and the Aspiring Entrepreneur. It distinguishes between those who are self-motivated and those who are waiting to be discovered, those who are happy and those who are unfulfilled. It aims to give you the tools to become more self-aware and happier and to find more meaning in your career. Ultimately, it is my hope that it inspires you to aggressively chase your dreams.

Part Three allows you to take the ideas of this book and make them your own. There is a worksheet to get you started (1) assessing where you are in your career and (2) understanding the actions you need to take to make a change. I've also included my personal worksheets, which I have filled out for different stages of my life and career, to show how goals and objectives can change over time. These completed worksheets are included in Appendix C.

Part 1

Why Work Isn't Working

1

Changing Work

Until now, companies, not employees, have been in control. There has been a surplus of workers, and companies have been able to call the shots about where people work and when. But the world of work is dramatically shifting. There is a huge shortage of talent coming.[1] What makes me say that? The population is growing, not shrinking, so why will we be faced with a talent shortage? Studies show that the supply of people able to understand and respond to business challenges will fall short of the rising demand for business change and growth. In Silicon Valley, and elsewhere, we have more technical jobs and fewer students graduating with the technical chops we need. We need deeper technical skills in order to keep up and remain competitive.

Work as we know it is such an oxymoron: we have record unemployment, yet companies can't find enough of the right talent. Some 22 percent of employers reported that despite an abundant labor pool, they still have positions for which they can't find qualified candidates. Some 48 percent of HR managers said that there was an area of their organization in which they lacked qualified workers.[2] The war for talent will do nothing but accelerate.

In a "do or die" economy, it's clear that companies that take a critical look at their traditional business practices and adopt more agile work models will be better equipped for the long haul. At the same time, with Millennials graduating and entering a brutal job market while Baby Boomers cannot afford to retire, competition has never been so stiff. This is further proof that evolving beyond the traditional models of work is becoming essential for survival. Workers who have the right skills and operate with a mind-set that they are CEOs of their own destinies are best positioned to be in high demand and will be afforded the most choice.

There's a lot of talk about having it all. And, quite frankly, I wish I could have done it all: I wish I could have stayed close to my family, seen them more often, and also have had an exciting and lucrative career that put meat and potatoes on the table. I did not see many choices available to me thirty years ago when I made my own career decisions.

But today, given the incredible advances in technology and the amazing way in which the world is connected, you have more choices. It is your responsibility to seize the opportunity by embracing the technological tools available to you. You can do more than you've ever dreamed. I call this thinking the Spirit of "And." Today, we no longer have to think in terms of either-or. We can have great family and personal lives AND have great careers. And many entrepreneurs with new technologies, companies, and services are enabling this phenomenon—many because they wanted to benefit from it as well.

The opportunity in front of us is exciting. It's inspiring. And it's going to continue. When things are out of whack, they are most ripe for disruption. It's also a time when immense value can be created. There has always been a gold rush to new frontiers, and time and again we've seen the way that uncertain times inspire young companies, leading them to replace and quickly exceed the value of old companies. What do Southwest, Cisco, and salesforce.com all have in common? They were all started in times that were difficult—in times that needed fixing—the exact time when we need innovation and the exact time when it flourishes.

I understand that change is hard. People resist disrupting the status quo. When we first built the railroads in this country, no one would ride, afraid their bodies would explode. I'm not asking you to hop on a runaway train, but I am asking you to think differently about work and to urge others to join you for the ride.

FREELANCE NATION 2.0

When I began my career, everyone "went" to work. It was long before the advent of the Internet and personal computers; you had to go to work to gain access to computing power. Only very select people could participate in remote access programs. Most computer centers had people on call 24/7. When there was a problem, they had to drive to the office and fix the problem on-site. There was no such thing as logging on remotely. Employees had to be at their desks to do work. Our inboxes were paper based. We had written phone memos, not voicemail, so in order to receive a call, we had to be at work. There weren't PCs that could be disconnected and taken home. People brought disks back and forth. At that time, it wasn't firewalls that protected the network; it was office walls, and if you weren't inside the office, you weren't able to work. The idea of "office hours" actually made sense. Today it's an outdated idea.

When I was building my career, I went west to Silicon Valley, and I still believe in the magic that makes it an epicenter of innovation. The pioneering companies that were founded there, the access to venture capital, the proximity to world-class universities with incredible engineering departments, and the amazing weather have given Silicon Valley an edge. Entrepreneurs are drawn to it, and for many it makes good sense to relocate there. There are of course other unique locales that draw workers for certain industries, such as Los Angeles for the entertainment industry or New York for finance. These places still reign as special, but they are edge cases. More and more, thanks to the Internet, videoconferencing, and mobile devices, you can be anywhere and do your job. Where you work can now be more of a choice. Some places still make good common sense—and will for some time—but the connections we can make through technology open up more choices for all of us.

Today people are moving around for jobs, but unlike in the past, they're not moving from location to location but from one job to another (sometimes in the course of a day). This is a growing trend. In December 2009, the number of people who declared themselves self-employed for "economic reasons" (citing "slack work" or "business conditions") more than doubled from pre-recession levels and reached almost 1.2 million.[3] A report based on research from the Massachusetts Institute of Technology estimated that freelance positions are expected to make up half of all new jobs added during the economic recovery.[4] However, this increase in freelancing is not all spurred by a down economy.

Federal statistics dating back to 2005 show that even at that time, one-third of the workforce (more than forty-two million Americans) already had part-time or temporary jobs. The same stats show that more than ten million were independent contractors.[5] This phenomenon has been brewing for some time—since the 1970s, according to Sara Horowitz of Freelancers Union. "What the recession shows is that people are just following the work," she says.[6]

In the future, it will make more sense to work on a project-by-project basis, similar to how crews work on movies: the best team is organized, and it is made up of individuals who work together for a set period of time and then, upon completion of the project, go their separate ways. In many industries, people will gain the opportunity to have many different jobs and many different employers, and therefore achieve much more personal freedom.

Although analysts have long viewed a "mobile workforce" as an economic strength, what is meant by that term needs to be updated and redefined. The mobile workforce I believe in is not made up of people moving to a different city or state to find work, but of people working from wherever they want. So, you can stay where you are or go where you want and still find the work that best suits you and your family. It may not be within driving distance—in fact, it may be better if it's not. The average person wastes the equivalent of eight weeks a year commuting. Imagine what we can do if we claim those weeks back. Even on the most micro level, we can eliminate one of the most stressful parts of every workday.

GETTING TO GREEN

Aside from the benefits that companies can unlock with new methods of working, and the increased peace and fulfillment those methods can bring individuals, there's additional room and reason for change: the environment.

We're pretty much all now in agreement that global warming isn't a conspiracy theory but a real problem for the future health of our planet. Scientists, engineers, and citizens are exploring ways to solve it, ranging from electric cars to renewable energy to geoengineering, but somehow we overlook changing something that is right in front of all of us. Our traditional model of work isn't just suffocating us; it's spewing hundreds of millions of tons of greenhouse gas emissions into the atmosphere every year and negatively impacting the planet.

Two-thirds of the electricity load in the United States is consumed by offices, according to the U.S. Green Business Council. Offices account for about 38 percent of all greenhouse gas emissions, and much of the office space we have is unoccupied. (Alternatively, home energy is much cheaper and much better utilized.) This is a growing problem. Over approximately the next twenty years, greenhouse gas emissions from offices are expected to grow faster than those in any other sector—about 1.8 percent per year.[7]

Commuting—something none of us enjoy anyway—is a big culprit as well. American workers spend on average forty minutes a day commuting (this equates to eight weeks a year spent in the car). In total this wastes more than 3.7 billion hours and 2.3 billion gallons of gas in one year.[8] What a toll for something most of us don't like doing—sitting in traffic!

I'm not a climatologist, so when it comes to really fixing the environmental crisis, I don't know if the answer rests on solar, wind, geothermal, nuclear, or some genius combination of these and new technologies yet to be discovered. But I do know that we can stop adding to the problem, simply by changing the outdated way we work. If we leverage today's technologies so that we don't need to commute and then log in endless hours in climate-controlled office parks, we could massively reduce our negative impact on the environment.

It's good news all around. As the carbon footprint gets smaller, the cost to businesses goes down as well. Real estate is expensive. The U.S. General Services Administration (GSA) finds the cost of accommodating the average federal worker to be $10,000 to $15,000 annually and that eliminating one hundred work spaces could save an organization more than $1 million a year.[9] Some companies have found ways to reduce their space and save costs. Unisys reduced its real estate costs by 87 percent through telecommuting (workshifting). About 25 percent of IBM's worldwide workers telecommute from home offices, saving the company $700 million in real estate costs.[10] Even the government is getting on board. By leveraging teleworking and "office hoteling," the U.S. Patent and Trademark Office got rid of three floors of office work space, and by enabling lawyers to reserve space in advance (allowing roughly five workers to share one office) the agency saves approximately $1.5 million annually in office rental costs.[11]

There was a telecommuting movement in the 1990s that gained popularity but ultimately resulted in failures. At that time, the technology was not yet advanced enough to support hoteling or desk sharing, and getting work done was inefficient. Today, new technology that allows increased collaboration remotely is powering this trend, and this movement is also being boosted by a new green consciousness.

There's much brouhaha about "green jobs," or those that arise from new clean-tech companies, created to help solve the climate crisis. I'm all for this—we need this kind of innovation, but the problem is that green jobs are hardly the economic cure-all they are often made out to be, as they account for only a small fraction of the U.S. workforce.

What about taking a different approach to green jobs? We can change the way people work to make all jobs more green and pursue this on a mass level. Everyone can make her job more "green" just by making a few changes that she'd probably prefer, such as working from home a few days a week. Even if you want to keep office space, there are ways to use it much more efficiently. Studies by the U.S. General Services Administration show that at any given time, over half the workspace in the United States and Europe is not being used. During typical working hours—between 8:00 AM and 5:00 PM—space is being used at only 35 to 50 percent of full capacity.[12] Companies that wise up to this reality win. We can start small, but even eliminating some of our dependence on office buildings will have a profound effect on our lives both in and out of business.

We are beginning to make incredible advances. As many of the millions of freelancers, independent contractors, at-home workers, and even traditional employees will tell you, getting a better job no longer requires picking up and moving to a new geography; it just involves adopting a new mind-set. Companies too are embracing change. IBM has evolved far beyond the company I once knew that had me moving back and forth throughout the country. As of 2011, 39 percent of IBM's employees worked from some type of a remote environment. It's a trend that's growing: IBM increased its 4:1 staff-to-desk ratio to an average of 12:1.[13]

2

Technology: Powering the Future of Work

During the gold rush of 1848, several hundred thousand people descended on California. Half of them came by sea, a journey that took five to eight months, and the rest came by land, crossing mountains and rivers in horse-drawn wagons. When railroads were built some twenty years later, the treacherous trip was cut to about seven days. When I went west, more than a hundred years later, during a different rush—one that mined silicon instead of gold—my family boarded an airplane and reached our destination in just five hours.

Technology. You have to love it. Today, no one would think of traveling across the country in a covered wagon, or even by railroad, when aviation allows us to fly at a fraction of the time and expense.

Yet when it comes to the way we work, we follow the same practices that were set fifty years ago. It's not that we don't have the technologies—just as we have airplanes, we have the tools to help us go farther faster, cheaper, and more easily than before—we just haven't advanced our management mind-set enough to properly adopt them.

It often frustrates me that we use these technologies in our daily lives—to share photos with friends, to play games online, to watch missed episodes of our favorite shows—but we don't use them to tackle the tougher stuff. We're not very good at using today's most trailblazing technology—the Internet—to make our careers more enriching and to make our families' lives better.

When it comes to work practices, we operate as if we're in the twentieth, not the twenty-first century. It's time to change our thinking. It's time to integrate new ways to disrupt—and advance—work. Understanding and embracing today's technical trends is the fastest way to travel to the career of your dreams.

INNOVATION DRIVES PRODUCTIVITY

I'm a bit of a tech geek, but I didn't grow up a tinkerer or a whiz-kid programmer. Curious minded, I was always thinking and wondering "What if ...?" or "Why did that happen?" On some level, I've been enamored with the power of new ideas since I was a child; and as time went by, I came to realize how dramatically different our world could be as a result.

This often occurred in the simplest ways. Growing up in Florida, my house had no air conditioning. The grueling experience of not having AC in South Florida in August cannot be overstated. I would sometimes sneak my pillow into the freezer so that I had something cold to put my head on. (My mom was not a big fan of this idea.) I was always in awe of the many advances that enriched our lives—for example, the advent of TV, then color TV, then cable, then HDTV ... and I can't wait for widespread adoption of 3D. I haven't been alone in my excitement; all of us embrace advances that make our lives better, more fun, and more entertaining. Quickly, we all wonder how we ever lived without them.

Of course, this is how technology develops. Although some ideas that look as though they will take hold instead fade away (for example, VHS and Betamax), others create or redefine entire industries, and before long the world looks totally different.

We often take technology's impact on business completely for granted, but it is technology that has caused business to evolve: creating it, changing it, advancing it. The AC I longed for growing up, the invention of Willis Carrier, soon became cheaper and more pervasive, and ultimately gave rise to Sun Belt economies. Such devices as the cash register, the typewriter, the copier, and the fax machine changed and created industries and allowed everything to move faster.

The greatest disrupter of all—until now—has been the computer. At IBM, I worked in the start-up division that eventually created the PC. I experienced the impact of that device by being both involved in its development and a user. At the risk of sounding like a dinosaur, in my early career, I used a typewriter. I loved the IBM Selectric because when I made a mistake and backtracked, it cleaned it up without my having to use white-out. When disks were introduced to store information, it was a massive improvement, as you didn't have to start each document anew. What a difference the personal computer made: with it, you could edit to your heart's content, share, distribute, and store freely.

As new applications came along, computing power increased exponentially. Word processing led to accounting and databases. Eventually the software and hardware improvements were made so quickly that they rapidly outstripped a user's ability to keep up with all the richness. Think about how few features most people use in Outlook, Excel, or PowerPoint. Today, this situation is even more confusing, as applications come and go faster than ever. Every week there is generally a new favored application on Apple's App Store, and every day we receive information or an invitation to view something through a service such as Dropbox, Evernote, or Creatley, apps that didn't exist a few years ago and now reign as key tools to increase people's productivity and collaboration capabilities.

Moore's Law, at its simplest, states that technology, specifically transistors on an integrated circuit, will always get smaller and double in number, and therefore result in more powerful semiconductors, every twenty-four months. We've seen this law proven time and time again as computing capacity becomes bigger, faster, and cheaper. The computer, now as a portal to the Internet, has allowed us to do things we never imagined, and we can do them all increasingly faster.

In this chapter, I will detail various technological trends ignited by the Internet, including the rapid adoption of mobile devices, the proliferation of applications and video, the advent of cloud computing, and the formation of online communities and ecosystems. Some of these trends are well known, but I believe we are still at the start of the changes to come. All the technology shifts cited here will continue to develop and become more pronounced in how they affect work. What we have seen is only the very beginning.

HARNESSING THE POWER OF THE WEB

The Internet has enabled us to do things we never dreamed possible. We've seen the advances technology brings to our everyday lives: we can pay bills online and shop 24/7, we don't need to wait for the morning newspaper to be delivered to the driveway when news comes online in real time, and we can check in for a flight online instead of waiting in line.

It seems difficult to remember, but prior to the Internet, most communication between individuals was done over the phone or via snail mail. Companies operated the same way unless you had a significant relationship, in which case there were dedicated circuits between your offices. Networks were most common between offices within a large corporation. They were proprietary and costly.

Email was originally a text-only medium and predated the Internet. In fact, email was a crucial application that helped create the need for the Internet. It started to exist in the consumer world when portal services and bulletin board services arrived in the late 1980s. In this paradigm, people could dial into a service and talk with one another over email, though the connection speeds were slow. What an incredible step it was to start sharing files with each other. As the Internet became the standard for connecting all of these disparate networks, it unleashed a torrent of innovation. As long as you could connect to the Internet and follow its protocols, it no longer mattered what type of computer you used. Geography was no longer a constraint. If you had a computer and were on the Internet, you could get to anyone else in the world—even people you didn't know—at the speed of light. You could talk, share documents, and collaborate with anyone, anywhere.

Still, as the logistics weren't particularly simple, mass adoption didn't occur at that time. It was rather difficult to look up different websites, and you had to be fairly tech savvy to do so. That changed with the invention of the web browser. Marc Andreessen, the visionary founder of Netscape, made the Internet usable for everyone by creating a simple way to find things on the web. The browser made it easy to search the web for websites and information. The browser later drove the development of the web as we know it and led to content (Yahoo!), to apps (eBay, Amazon), to search (Google, Yahoo!), and to social (Facebook, Twitter). All of these innovations created a truly synergistic capability, which only continues to get stronger.

The growth of the Internet and the availability of high-speed connectivity to most places in the world have created profound

Technology Kick-Starts Industry Innovation

Advances in the Internet, devices, and mobile technology have enabled you to watch content—movies, TV shows, web videos—on your terms, wherever you are and on whatever device you'd like to use. TiVo first made the whole process of time shifting and watching shows on your schedule ridiculously easy, and now on-demand video streaming is commonplace. YouTube first popularized the advent of user-generated content, which opened content generation immensely.

Another industry that's advanced with technology is travel. GPS devices (in cars, handhelds, and smartphones) make getting lost dramatically harder to do. I use my smartphone and apps like Waze to learn about accidents or road closures and to be given options about how to minimize a delay. In a similar vein, the way we research and book trips is entirely different. Next-generation travel sites like Hipmunk (disclosure: I've invested in this company) display flight search results in an easy-to-view, easy-to-understand information-rich timeline and show hotel search results on a map, making the whole process of planning a trip easy and agony free.

changes for work. Over two billion people use broadband Internet, up from perhaps fifty million a decade ago.[1] Employees no longer have to be in the office to communicate. The Internet eliminates the need to be tied to one geographical location. Workers can work from wherever they want.

This idea of working from anywhere became a reality when enabled by advances in security. Solutions like virtual private networks allow employees to access the company from wherever they are just as securely as if they were on the corporate network. The proliferation of laptops and tablets and the rapid adoption of the mobile Internet have given us freedom from working within an office that was unimaginable only a few years ago.

THE WORLD GOES MOBILE

When the personal computer became portable with the emergence of laptops, it was revolutionary: you could work on planes, take your device on trips, use the same machine at work and at home. Similarly, cell phones were once as big as bricks, but they helped people stay available and in touch regardless of whether they were at their desk or at home.

Smartphones take both of these trends to the next level. We now can carry a device around at all times that has more computing power than all of NASA had in 1969, the year it sent man to the moon.[2] Depending on how it's configured, it lets people and services know exactly where you are, and in some cases, it allows services to tailor a unique offering solely for you. Your smartphone is also a camera (in many cases capable of capturing video), and many of them can make videoconference calls directly between two smartphones.

The mobile market is exploding, and according to some experts, it's driving the biggest behavior transformation we've ever seen.[3] In the coming years, there will be more mobile devices than computing devices by a long shot. Many emerging countries like India and China jumped straight to wireless (mobile) capability. In the wireless world, though, as of 2012 only one-quarter of phones sold were smartphones, so we are still a long way from where we are going. Over the next ten years, according to Internet visionary turned venture capitalist Marc Andreessen, it's expected that at least five billion people worldwide will own smartphones, giving every individual with such a phone instant access to the Web.[4] This has huge implications for work.

WORK MIGRATES TO THE CLOUD

We all know how the Internet has changed the lives of consumers: it's changed how we communicate, how we shop, how we meet people. It's changed things for businesses too. How software is developed and deployed for Internet platforms is dramatically different from what it is for enterprise platforms. Historically, in enterprises, you deployed in phases over years; you had to implement your own centers and buy hardware and software up front. Now the enterprise world is moving to the Internet platform model. This is generally known as cloud computing, meaning that information is stored in online servers, as opposed to hardware on your premises. Often people talk about the cost and speed advantages of the cloud. Those advantages are real, but the greatest of them is the speed with which you can innovate once there.

In my newest endeavor, the Webb Investment Network (WIN), which invests in start-up companies, we run things entirely

Starting Your Own Business from Your Laptop

It's easier to start a company today than it ever was before. In the past, an Internet start-up required all sorts of significant technology investments, including purchasing servers and bandwidth as well as hiring the IT experts to take care of it.* It was not unusual for start-up costs to add up to millions of dollars. Today they're a tiny fraction of that. There are many reasons for the change, most of which are a direct result of the Internet and web-based services. Amazon Web Services, for example, has been a great enabler. It's elastic; you can rent time on the server and scale it up or down. Google App Engine and salesforce's Force.com have also greatly reduced infrastructure costs. "There is no barrier to entry any more for new ideas," says Andy Bechtolsheim (cofounder of Sun and one of the first investors in Google).** Another phenomenon that has reduced marketing costs is social networking platforms. Viral platforms like Twitter and Facebook have allowed us to reach audiences and market products and services in an entirely new way.

*Benjamin Black and Vijay Gill, "Web Infrastructure and a Startup Funding Manifesto," GigaOM, January 11, 2009, http://gigaom.com/2009/01/11/fail-fast-a-startup-funding-manifesto/.

**Barb Darrow, "Bechtolsheim: AWS, Open Source Rewrite Rules for Startups," GigaOM, November 10, 2011, http://gigaom.com/2011/11/10/arista-roadmap-2011/.

in the cloud. Everyone who works at WIN is an independent contractor. We have an office, but we go in only twice a week; the rest of the time, everyone works from wherever he or she wants, such as hotels, coffee shops, home, or the office of one of the companies we've invested in. We share documents through a service called Dropbox, track action items through a service called Smartsheet, and manage our deal flow through a custom cloud application. Although we are geographically dispersed, everyone knows exactly what everyone else is working on. When we do get together in person, we are able to cover things very quickly.

POWERING A GLOBAL COMMUNITY

With global access enabled by the Internet, you are no longer restricted by your geography. Perhaps eBay offers the best example of this. eBay lets people hunt for treasures across the globe, not only at places within driving distance. It also connects people with common interests and passions.

That's been a game changer for consumers, but what eBay also sparked was a new way to work. As of 2012, there were more than one million people who make a full or part-time living on eBay, most from their own home. Selling everything from antiques to toys, from makeup to crafts, from cars to collectibles, many eBay entrepreneurs have found doing what they love to also be a lucrative profession.

We've seen the same type of community formation take place in other industries. LiveOps, where I am the chairman, is one such example. LiveOps runs a virtual call center, where twenty thousand agents work as independent contractors from their own homes and on their own schedules. Technology, especially cloud-based solutions, has enabled this community. All of the virtual learning, work scheduling, team meetings, and feedback sessions take place on LiveOps' cloud-based technology platform. All the software is accessible right over the Internet, and all the calls are routed using Voice over Internet Protocol (VoIP)—technology that didn't exist fifteen years ago.

I didn't start LiveOps; I joined when it was six years old, and became enamored with its model based on meritocracy, in which the best-performing agents receive the most calls and, as a result, make the most money. The agents love their role because they get to work on what they want, when they want. The platform is also great for our customers, as our results-based routing technology sends calls to the most appropriate agent. This model worked so well that LiveOps' cloud contact center technology is now being used by large global brands such as salesforce.com and Symantec to match the best agents with customers, regardless of location and time zone. More and more companies are adopting this practice, finding talent through sites like oDesk, Elance, CrowdFlower, and Samasource and distributing work in a new way—one based on talent rather than presence.

New video technologies fuel work collaboration among people who are dispersed in different locations. Technologies from Polycom PictureTel, Cisco, and Hewlett-Packard and free services like FaceTime, Skype, and GoToMeeting have revolutionized how we meet with people who are not in the same building. It's also revolutionizing customer service departments and changing the way companies engage with consumers. Salesforce.com's service cloud relies on video technology to connect customers with agents who can "look" at what is wrong and instruct the customer through the right steps to a resolution.

I don't want to advocate that video replaces the need to get together and make more human connections with people. There is something magical about being physically present, and even the most advanced technology in the world can't replace this human need and the connection that we all crave. But we can use technology to replace the encounters that are not necessary and to improve the ones that are inefficient.

WORK IS THE NEXT KILLER APP

What does all this—mobile, cloud, social, platforms, and applications—have to do with work and with you?

In one word, everything. You can think differently about how and when you work, and you should. Technology, and applications of this technology, will continue to improve and evolve, providing unprecedented, global access to information, individuals, training, and opportunities. But perhaps most important of all, technology provides individuals with unequaled flexibility. You don't have to be bound to geography anymore, and you don't have to be tied to one company anymore.

The price of admission to this new world is that you have to be excellent—it's a meritocracy, in which the best people rise to the top. But if you embrace that philosophy, you have more choice than ever before. This is not just something limited to where I live in Silicon Valley; with the rapid adoption of cloud computing and mobile devices, technology is a game changer around the globe. Politicians, including Cory Booker, mayor of Newark, New Jersey, have been promoting technology as the crucial key for change. "In the 21st century, if you're looking for work, you shouldn't have to search in the same old places and, once hired, you shouldn't have to clock in and clock out in the same old ways," said Booker in his 2011 State of the City Address. "We should be able to go beyond bricks and mortar and draw upon the information and communication technology of today."[5]

As everything goes digital, new technologies such as mobile, social, and video all have far-reaching ramifications on work. We don't have to go to an office, and we can engage in self-directed, continuous education. And good news for entrepreneurs (what most young people want to be): today, a company can start up within a week. (It used to take a year.)

I am reminded of this wherever I turn. Recently, my wife, Irene, and I were having dinner at a local restaurant, and we began chatting with our server, a young woman named Kathryn Medina. Kathryn had graduated from college a few years before and landed a good job, but her employer had been struggling in the ailing economy. As a result, her company ultimately laid off 85 percent of the staff—an event that led her to waiting tables to make ends meet.

At the same time that she accepted the waitressing job, Kathryn also gave thought to what she really wanted to do and began to work with three friends doing web design for local businesses. "We created the jobs we needed," she said.

The partners contributed their unique skills and passions— graphic design, marketing and writing, web design, and photography—and within a few months their endeavor, called Squiber, became a profitable one-stop shop that helped small businesses create their online identity. They didn't lease office space, and the four business partners worked from home. "As long as I have a computer and Internet connection, I can work anywhere," Kathryn explained. She also explained how these were her final days as a waitress: she was now earning enough through Squiber to support herself—and to pursue one of her lifelong dreams, to travel throughout South America.

What inspires me most about Kathryn's story is not only how she symbolizes what's possible with new thinking and new technology in this Age of Entrepreneurship but also how she took it a step further, creating a way to make work *work* for her. She earned her undergraduate degree in international business and always had the bug to travel. Now, living as the CEO of her own destiny, she is making her dream a reality and planning to live in South America for six months. She'll work on her goal of becoming fluent in Spanish and at the same time contribute to Squiber, using Skype to talk to her business partners and clients as well as a site called join.me, which will allow her to share her computer screen with colleagues as well as gain access to their screens. With easy-to-use and affordable services like these, collaboration from anywhere has never been simpler.

Kathryn's story shows how the old "safety net" of a corporate job is not really much of a safety net at all. Not only is it precarious in these challenging economic times, but it also can tie you down and even choke your dreams. For Kathryn, being let go by her employer and taking a waitressing job as her own safety net was the best thing that could have happened: it set her free to pursue what she really wanted. "This has been my dream since I was a little girl," she told me. "I wouldn't have been able to do it unless we started Squiber."

Part 2

Reframing How We Think About Work

3

The Framework

I've always enjoyed coaching. After my dreams of becoming a Major League ballplayer were dashed, I wanted to be a sports coach or a teacher—both jobs that mentor people. Early on in my career, I received the benefits of being mentored. Advice from someone who had been there before was invaluable. As my career progressed, people began to seek me out as a mentor. I hosted fireside chats for eBay employees who came looking for leadership development. I talked about the value of infusing integrity in everything you do and the importance of aiming high, but what I found most of all was that people were looking for direction in how to live more fulfilling lives.

They wanted to work, but they wanted it to be fulfilling and worth the sacrifices of missing time with their families. People wanted more than monetary gain; they wanted meaning. Work, as they were experiencing it, wasn't providing that. I spent time thinking about what was wrong with work—I found a lot that was—and I began thinking about what it was that made people unsatisfied and how to solve for those issues. The following framework is the culmination of this investigation and, I hope, will serve as a template for you as you begin to rework how you think about your career and your life.

The following four-frame chart identifies four different philosophies around work—Company Man or Woman, CEO of Your Own Destiny, Disenchanted Employee, and Aspiring Entrepreneur.

The Framework: Where Do You See Yourself?

	Paternalistic Era	The Age of Entrepreneurship
Meritocracy: feels personally invested, proactive, positive, willing	**Frame 1** **Company Man or Woman** • You are a high achiever. • You have a great attitude. • You are on a promotion track. • You have only as much future as the company you are with. **Recommendation:** *Continue your emphasis on high performance, but broaden your view of your career beyond the constraints of any one company.*	**Frame 2** **CEO of Your Own Destiny** • You are highly successful. • You are self-aware. • You love the freedom this choice has given you. • You opt in to being fully on the team every day. • You work to build a network outside the office "walls." • You have great and fulfilling career options. **Recommendation:** *You can work for yourself or a corporation and still be the CEO of Your Own Destiny. This is the sweet spot for the future of work.*
Entitlement: feels deserving, frustrated, critical	**Frame 3** **Disenchanted Employee** • You are waiting to be discovered or recognized. • You can't understand why others don't understand how good you are. • You are not progressing in your career at the speed you expected. • You believe your circumstances to be someone else's problem. **Recommendation:** *Take a meaningful look at what you want to achieve and the steps you will take to achieve it.*	**Frame 4** **Aspiring Entrepreneur** • You fully embrace controlling your own destiny. • You don't have enough work to do on the terms you are willing to do it. • You may not be addressing the gaps between your desires and your skills. **Recommendation:** *Reassess your value proposition to understand why your view of your value is not aligned with your current environment; make appropriate course corrections.*

As workplaces shift, in some ways Frame 1, the Company Man or Woman, is a difficult role, if only because corporate stability is hard to find. Frame 2—CEO of Your Own Destiny—is the sweet spot that more people need to know about, where they are not dependent on a corporation or hindered by their own frustrations. As this is where most workplaces are headed—there is no longer any job security—this is the mind-set individuals need to adopt to be successful today and in the future. This is the true path to security in the new Age of Entrepreneurship. Frame 3, the Disenchanted Employee, is the antithesis of Frame 1; this individual is not only still working for "The Man" but also assigning the employer too much responsibility for his personal happiness and fulfillment. Frame 4 is the dark side of Frame 2; this individual understands and values personal freedom, but she is not yet succeeding in her goals.

I began my own experiences within this framework as a Company Man (Frame 1), and my career has been a journey to becoming a CEO of My Own Destiny (Frame 2). There were times in any day or week that I could live momentarily in Frame 3. For example, at Quantum, I had been promoted to director of IT. It was my second promotion in two years; however, I didn't feel that my position aptly represented what I was doing. I knew that the role as head of IT at a company our size should have carried the title of vice president, and likely of CIO. Still, I happily accepted the job even with the discrepancy because I knew it was a big step up for me. Later, after we acquired Digital Computer's disk drive business, a billion-dollar business with thousands of people, I was tasked with leading the massive and challenging integration. I devised a plan, which carried significant risk and was reviewed by the board and a seasoned professional who was supportive of my approach. My boss told me that if I pulled the project off, I could definitely become a VP. The project went very smoothly. Upon completion, my boss said, "Thanks," gave my team and me a bonus, and said, "I expect to promote you next year." I walked out of the room in Frame 3, disenchanted for sure. I felt that I had been promised a promotion if I delivered this massive, risky project. However, what I received was little more than a pat on the back and a "You're still not quite ready." Ironically, that night I received a call from a headhunter for a VP and CIO role at Bay Networks. I left Quantum within a few months to take that job.

When I became a product manager at Thomas-Conrad, I was living in Frame 4—and I knew it. I understood that at the start of a new job, you didn't quite yet have all the tools and experiences needed to do the job well. Often, the economics are such that one needs to take a haircut financially. (I did that in a big way as I went to a white-collar job at IBM to do computer security, and where I lost overtime and other special perks that I had received as a security guard. I had to live solely on a base salary. My job content and future prospects were great as a result of the move, but my immediate financial situation took a hit, and I took a nights-and-weekend job at a department store.) By the time I got to be director of product management at Thomas-Conrad, I was in a better negotiating position, as I had accumulated more accomplishments and gained a reputation for having a great work ethic. Still, I had never been a product manager and had a lot to learn. The CEO, with whom I had worked at IBM, was willing to pay me for my track record at producing results and for my work ethic as opposed to my current product management skills. At that point, I was in Frame 4 and worked hard to bring my skills up to speed so that my knowledge would match my compensation. I achieved this after about six months of challenging work and moved into Frame 1, enjoying working for this company and delivering results for it. Unfortunately, the CEO who hired me lost his job later that year. The company founder returned as the CEO and told me I was one of the most highly paid guys in the company and that I therefore wouldn't get a raise for a couple of years. At that time, I had four small children, had produced significant results, and felt far more comfortable in my capability. Without recognition of my efforts and validation of my success from the company, I started treading into Frame 3, feeling unappreciated and unhappy. As a result, I searched for a higher-paying job in product management in the same city. I declined an attractive offer after the CEO at Thomas-Conrad asked me to stay. I agreed, but I never really got out of Frame 3 and back above the line, and I left the company within a year.

Where do you see yourself in this framework right now? If you are in Frame 1—a high achiever, but you measure success by your title or the size of your office—you can benefit from accepting more responsibility for your future and recognizing that you, not your employer, are in charge.

The issue with Frame 1 is that you are always only as good as the company you are with. That's a problem when you are a star performer at Lehman Brothers or Bear Stearns or a company that goes bust overnight. The hard-working attorneys at Dewey & LeBoeuf, the once-esteemed giant law firm, had their careers and finances upended, regardless of their own personal performance, when the firm spiraled out of control and collapsed in 2012. Employees across the entire organization were left scrambling for paychecks and jobs—and trying to evade blame.[1]

Even on a less extreme scale, every employee is somewhat at the mercy of the company. You will be promoted when the company decides, be moved where it determines, and work on projects that it sees as most suitable for your skill set. There's also an inherent conflict with this setup: employers do what's best for the company, which is not always what's best for the employee.

Maybe you identify with Frame 3. All of us have days when we feel unappreciated, but taking a victim's perspective can be dangerous. There are many scenarios that can spark this sentiment. Maybe you were passed up for a promotion you feel you deserved. Maybe someone else—someone you deem less qualified—got that promotion. Instead of watching other people run up the stairs and hoping they stumble back down, figure out how they got there, and start running harder yourself. Also, I've found that it is very hard to run fast when you're constantly looking around to see where everyone else is going.

I remember joining eBay when there were a couple hundred people. Many of those folks thought we had gotten too big. I told them companies either grow or shrink, that they don't stay the same—success is about growth. It's not about looking back; it's about going forward. When I left eBay, we were employing over ten thousand people.

I think many founders live in Frame 2, and then when their companies are purchased, they seldom move to Frame 1 but more often move to Frame 3, where they do not feel as in control of their destinies as they did when they were running their own show. They often complain about how slowly big companies move and how hard it is to get things done.

In mergers and acquisitions, the acquiring companies are buying products, customers, and people, so they try hard to incent founders to stay. One of the ways they do this is by giving extra compensation, bonuses, and stock in the new company, but to some entrepreneurs, whether or not they already made significant money, this may not be enough. Financial incentives pale in importance to the control and freedom these entrepreneurs relinquish. Many see their time at the acquiring company as an "opportunity cost," and they are soon burning to start their own thing again. I don't think they intend to feel this way; it is just something that happens to entrepreneurial people, and many leave and seek to get back to Frame 2, where they will feel more in control.

Sometimes the executives of the acquired companies also experience a bit of "organ rejection" when internal employees become jealous of this new group of folks who haven't yet accomplished that much yet at the organization, but who receive special perks, while they are charged with keeping the mother ship running. These people often make life difficult and adamantly push the company rules, which creates a divide. For example, when eBay acquired PayPal, we had to decide which culture would prevail. Would we change the logo? Would we adopt PayPal's policy of giving free food to employees? (We kept PayPal employees whole by continuing this and added some perks for eBay employees to match it.) We didn't do everything right and lost a lot of PayPal executives during the transition. Later, when eBay acquired Skype, Shopping.com, and StubHub, it kept these entities largely separate so that they could grow on their own. Similarly, when salesforce.com acquired Radian6 and Heroku, it allowed them to operate somewhat autonomously so that the entrepreneurial spirit still remained and the talent stayed.

Sometimes entrepreneurs are energized by the opportunity to play in a larger field—I recently met someone who sold his business to Yahoo! who felt this way—but too often, I see a lot of the founders leave as soon as their contract allows, not because the new company is not great, but because founders love doing their own thing and feel much more personal fulfillment when they're back in Frame 2.

Another situation that breeds this brand of work crankiness arises when someone has been doing a job for too long, which makes it feel stale, and the employee begins to feel disenchanted. It's important to always be growing and taking on new responsibilities and roles to avoid this. There are several ways to get boxed into Frame 3, but what's most important is to get out of it. Frame 3, like Frame 1, cedes control to someone else; it embraces an attitude that someone else is responsible for your success or failure. However, that worldview does not reflect today's reality, in which everyone has an ownership stake in his or her success. If you are living in Frame 3, you must start to seek new inspiration to make you feel empowered.

Maybe you associate more with Frame 4. You are entrepreneurial and are charting your own way, but it hasn't all come together yet. Or maybe you think you are worth more than what you are being paid. You have goals, but you aren't achieving all of them. If you are living in Frame 4, you know what you want—and what you think you are worth—but there's a discrepancy with what others think. In short, your opinion of yourself is ahead of the way others see you.

Self-confidence will take you far, but you can't get ahead without aligning everyone with you and convincing them of your abilities. Take a deeper look at your skills and abilities and determine where the gaps are that are preventing you from getting to where you know you should be. A mentor can be pivotal in helping you identify what you should work on so that you can connect to what you want. Another option is to live in a hybrid world where you are practicing and developing the skills that will let you break into Frame 2 while securing the economics you need from the traditional relationship of Frame 1. I remember in the early 1990s when I was being recruited to an IT job in Colorado. It would be a great place to live, and the job carried an enticing title and benefits, but the company was not on the leading edge of technology, which is where I always wanted to be. I told my wife that I would take it for the sake of the family, as I thought we could have a better house and potentially a better life in Boulder, but that I was not sure I would be fulfilled not pushing the envelope in my career. Even then I was rebelling against living in Frame 1. We decided that the benefits did not outweigh being tied to this one company. Had I taken the job, however, I would have been adopting a hybrid interim approach.

Although this framework divides work into four distinct states, no one is likely to stay in one frame his or her entire career. I spent the beginning of my career firmly entrenched in Frame 1. I was a Company Man, comforted by the security of a paternalistic company. I followed the career trajectory IBM devised for me, and I was rewarded for my loyalty with promotions and bigger offices. I evolved into Frame 2 when I left IBM and decided I would no longer cede control to a company. However, I don't think I embraced all the attributes of Frame 2 until much more recently, when I left the trappings of a traditional day job and began to work on my own terms (where and when I wanted). There were times on my journey to Frame 2 when I fell below the line into Frames 3 and 4, and I know the difficulties and unhappiness associated with them.

I have always looked at the careers of people I respected and admired for guidance and found that many of these role models also vacillated between frames. Marc Benioff, a legendary entrepreneur and the founder of salesforce.com, the most innovative company in the world according to *Forbes*, spent more than thirteen years as a poster child for Frame 1. He was incredibly loyal to his employer, Oracle, where he worked from college graduation and rose up the corporate ranks and was a quintessential Company Man until he had an idea that he believed in so strongly that he left the security of his executive salary and stock options behind to take a bet on it. There were times in the early days of salesforce.com—when people did not understand or accept his new idea to deliver business applications over the Internet, or in the cloud—that Marc was living in Frame 4. Marc is a visionary, and he knew where he was going (and where enterprise software was going), but his view was not aligned with the commonly held worldview. In time—and with the help of some very effective marketing and education—Marc and salesforce.com bridged those gaps. Today, Marc is the epitome of Frame 2. He is pursuing his dream of being an entrepreneur, and he's also been able simultaneously to pursue his passion for making a difference in the world through his incredible commitment to philanthropy.

Today's generation pursues entrepreneurship completely differently from the way Marc did. Eddy Lu, the cofounder of Grubwithus, a great start-up that has created a social service to meet people over a meal, never felt content in Frame 1. In fact, he told me that he and his cofounder landed great corporate jobs out of college, but they never liked them.

When Eddy graduated from the University of California, Berkeley, in 2003, there wasn't a buzzing start-up scene. Google had not yet gone public, and Microsoft was a place where everyone wanted to work. Eddy took a job at Deloitte, a great gig, but one that he said left him "unfulfilled." "I was executing someone's orders; I was a minor cog in a grand scheme," he says. "It was not too fulfilling, and I wanted to work on a smaller team and do something more fun and meaningful." Eddy moved on to a job at Lehman Brothers, where he had more responsibility, but where he was turned off by the strict culture and the fact that he was "still a cog even though it was a bigger cog." In looking to do something that felt more meaningful, he started to think about entrepreneurial opportunities with his roommate. They bought a whiteboard and started to devise various plans. Short of the big idea but long on inspiration, they quit their jobs and decided they would figure out the next right move. (Frame 4, here they come!)

They stressed over what to tell their parents, who were of a different generation and proud of their respectable and seemingly stable jobs. (Obviously Lehman Brothers didn't turn out to be stable, but no one knew what would come at the time.) "What are you doing with your life?" Eddy's father questioned.

"Some people say they tried every business under sun, and we really did," says Eddy, describing his various entrepreneurial endeavors, including an import–export business, a retail tea effort, and a golf apparel fashion line. (He took sewing and color classes to prepare for that one.) Eddy also sold underwear at the night markets in Asia and attempted to create iPhone games. He eventually came upon a cream puff franchise, Beard Papa's; he bought into the business and opened a store in Los Angeles.

Though successful—he and his roommate eventually opened four cream puff stores—the franchise business didn't allow Eddy to become CEO of his own destiny. He used social media sites like Facebook to attract attention and clientele, created his own website, and put his own pictures on the menu, but these tactics were not included in the marketing plan of the franchisor, and Eddy began to get into trouble for not sticking to the rules.

(Franchisors are notoriously old world and paternalistic.) Eddy was ordered to stop these efforts or his contract would be terminated. "We still felt like we were being controlled by a corporate environment; it was supposed to be like we were our own bosses, but it wasn't really," he says.

At this point, Eddy was stuck in Frame 4. He had a big dream and a lot of drive, but it wasn't all adding up. Living in a new city—the last franchise they opened was in Chicago—Eddy found himself alone with no family and few friends, and this was when his greatest entrepreneurial epiphany struck. He couldn't just go up to people and ask them to be a friend—"they would run away," he laughs—but what if he found a way to recreate a dinner party environment, a climate that enabled new people to meet casually and ignite new friendships? What if he created dinner parties for the masses? After all, everyone needed to eat, but with people often moving to new cities or traveling for work or fun, they didn't have anyone to eat with. Initially, Eddy and his business partner launched a social site to invite people to eat with them, and it resonated, so they built a platform to enable anyone to host a meal. (Grubwithus has deals with the restaurants and makes money by receiving a cut of the total for the meals.) They now have meals in more than fifty cities and have hosted more than ten thousand meals.

Eddy started in Frame 3 (he had a corporate job, but he never liked it); spent a lot of time in Frame 4, where he had a vision but couldn't get it aligned with the market or backers; and ultimately made his way to Frame 2, the promised land. Eddy learned to rely on himself as he carved his path to Frame 2. (This included giving up the trappings of a steady income and even living in his car while he was raising money from business incubator Y Combinator.) I am certain he will live in Frame 2 most of the time. (Disclosure: I have invested in Grubwithus.) It's not always easy, but for Eddy, living in Frame 2 is more rewarding. "Being responsible for your own destiny has its own stresses, struggles, and responsibility. It's a lot more work and pressure, but I'm happier. It's my own baby, and I want to see it succeed. I work harder than I ever did, but I don't think about it as work because it's fun to me, and I want to make something cool."

———————

What frame do you live in? The fact is, you might not fit squarely into one frame, and you might move from one frame to another and even shift around from one day to the next. That's okay. There is supposed to be fluidity to the frames. You will be in different frames at different points in your career, and you can find ways to move out of one and into another. What's most important, however, is deciding what frame you want to be in—and then, with the help of this book—determining how to get there.

Please remember that all worthwhile change takes time, hard work, and patience. My hope is that this methodology helps you to engage thoughtfully in the process of change and to create positive changes over time.

4

Frame 1: The Company Man or Woman

After I graduated from college, IBM offered me a job as a security guard working in the lobby and protecting the grounds of its Rochester campus. I thought that meant New York. It wasn't. It was Rochester, Minnesota.

I visited Minnesota during the summer and made note of the beautiful rolling hills, the polite Midwesterners, and the plugs in the cars so they could be started on cold days. (Having grown up in Florida, this last part was a bad sign.)

But this was a job, and that was what I needed. There weren't any work opportunities at IBM in Boca Raton, which was close to my hometown and my extended family. Moving away made sense: I was excited to have gainful employment, and this gig was an improvement over my previous posts in pest control, landscaping, and working at a mattress factory.

I packed everything up and headed northwest to Minnesota. I soon became busy with work and a new life, but there were challenges that stemmed from living far from family and friends.

The phone bills, for example, were atrocious. (This was before cell phones and unlimited calling plans.)

After nine months with IBM, I was presented with an opportunity to become a systems engineer, for which I would have received in-depth training in engineering, leading to a job installing and selling computers to customers. It was an exciting opportunity. However, I turned it down because it meant a ninety-minute commute twice a day. Soon I was offered another opportunity: a new facility was being opened in Charlotte, North Carolina. I asked only one question: "Is it south of the Mason-Dixon line?" I moved to Charlotte, and as soon as a job came up in Boca Raton—five years later—I eagerly accepted it.

We used to joke that IBM stood for "I've Been Moved," as my many relocations were more the norm than the exception. But finally, I was where I wanted to be. Home.

I spent a decade at IBM. Now, upon reflection, it boggles my mind to think about how we measured success when I was an executive. There was a whole hierarchy of "achievements" that demonstrated you had made it, from your job title to the years-of-service badge on your ID card to the location of your office to the number of ceiling tiles you had. (More tiles equaled more status.) Wood furniture, believe it or not, was another status symbol. (At one major magazine, friends tell me management would demonstrate the significance of your contributions by whether or not shrimp was served at your farewell party. No shrimp, your leaving was no real loss to the company.)

This was what my life was like in Frame 1, life as a Company Man. In hindsight, some of it seems asinine, but it wasn't all bad. With a paternalistic culture came defined ways to cultivate people. There were development plans, coaches, high-performer tracks, and management schools. Maybe everyone accused you of having a lobotomy when you came back, but there was a certain comfort in having a company care for you—of having them "groom" you to become an executive. (At many companies, including some large professional services firms, this was literal, including telling men they couldn't have facial hair. Imagine that happening today?)

I had been back in Florida for five years when IBM decided to shut down the manufacturing plant in Boca Raton. They offered anyone willing to leave a sweet deal: two years' salary, two years of benefits, and $25,000, but I didn't even consider it. I didn't want to leave IBM. I was firmly entrenched in the Company Man square on the framework.

My wife had other plans, however. I had met Irene at IBM, and we got married in 1986. In 1988, she was pregnant with our daughter, and she thought the package was too compelling to pass up. If she was going to leave, I decided I would too. I left IBM after eleven years.

With that move I also left behind my belief in the paternalistic company. I recognized that no corporation should or could take care of me forever. At first this was a scary realization. But as time wore on, I realized how empowering and liberating it was to view myself as the CEO of my own destiny. This didn't mean that I could never work for anyone else again. In fact, I would spend the next several decades working for other companies ... but I was the one in charge of my fate. This was perhaps the most influential epiphany of my career.

The Framework: Where Do You See Yourself?

	Paternalistic Era	The Age of Entrepreneurship
Meritocracy: feels personally invested, proactive, positive, willing	**Frame 1** **Company Man or Woman** • You are a high achiever. • You have a great attitude. • You are on a promotion track. • You have only as much future as the company you are with. **Recommendation:** *Continue your emphasis on high performance, but broaden your view of your career beyond the constraints of any one company.*	**Frame 2** **CEO of Your Own Destiny** • You are highly successful. • You are self-aware. • You love the freedom this choice has given you. • You opt in to being fully on the team every day. • You work to build a network outside the office "walls." • You have great and fulfilling career options. **Recommendation:** *You can work for yourself or a corporation and still be the CEO of Your Own Destiny. This is the sweet spot for the future of work.*
Entitlement: feels deserving, frustrated, critical	**Frame 3** **Disenchanted Employee** • You are waiting to be discovered or recognized. • You can't understand why others don't understand how good you are. • You are not progressing in your career at the speed you expected. • You believe your circumstances to be someone else's problem. **Recommendation:** *Take a meaningful look at what you want to achieve and the steps you will take to achieve it.*	**Frame 4** **Aspiring Entrepreneur** • You fully embrace controlling your own destiny. • You don't have enough work to do on the terms you are willing to do it. • You may not be addressing the gaps between your desires and your skills. **Recommendation:** *Reassess your value proposition to understand why your view of your value is not aligned with your current environment; make appropriate course corrections.*

THE RISE OF THE PATERNALISTIC COMPANY

IBM was the quintessential paternalistic company, and during my employment there it was an admired company—a company that employees flocked to and that other employers modeled themselves after. In many ways, it was the epitome of what work meant at the time.

To understand this better, and to see how people get into Frame 1—and why so many of them become entrenched there—it's helpful to understand the history of work. Although today there's little reason to "go" to work or be tethered to a certain geography, this idea certainly made sense a hundred years ago. Indeed, it was the only way.

Although nine out of ten white males worked for themselves in the United States in 1890,[1] the Industrial Revolution that came in the nineteenth century transformed everything about how we worked. As factories were built and industries were established, people left their rural homes and moved to burgeoning cities. Americans began to work for companies and seek employment outside rural communities. There was a defined hierarchy between the laborers and the managers. Tremendous advances, such as the assembly line, made workers more efficient and made companies more productive.[2] The new discipline required dramatically changed the way people worked: employees went to work for set hours and were paid set salaries.

It was this same shift that also laid the groundwork for companies to become paternalistic. Anyone familiar with Upton Sinclair's *The Jungle* is well aware of the horror stories that defined factory life at the turn of the twentieth century. Factories were sweatshops, where new immigrants who came expecting to find opportunity and streets paved with gold, instead worked long hours under very tough conditions. Workers soon began to respond. The Ford Motor Company saw its employee turnover rate for assembly line workers reach 370 percent in 1913. The working conditions were so terrible that 71 percent of new hires quit after less than five days on the line.[3]

Workers and muckraking journalists began to organize and demand changes—and they received some. By 1916, the Adamson Act established eight hours as the basic workday and required higher overtime pay for longer hours. Labor unions came into existence and grew rapidly during this time.

Corporate culture began to change in reaction to the difficulties of the turn-of-the-century workplace. Management offered better pay and benefits to retain the best employees and to reduce workers' motivation to join the growing labor movement. Companies, including Ford, created reward systems that offered compelling gifts in that era, such as gold watches and grandfather clocks, to encourage employees to stay.[4]

In the 1920s, as the Supreme Court reversed state laws that allowed for factory inspections and other protections for workers—and as labor unrest spread as unions fought for reforms like the eight-hour day—some corporations stepped up their paternalistic efforts, offering benefits ranging from health care to organized recreation.[5] They began setting up formal "employee representation" systems for workers to make their voices heard. The New Deal, passed in the 1930s in response to the Great Depression, provided workers with important protections and benefits.

Weekly hours continued to decline during the first third of the century, and after World War II, the length of the workweek stabilized at around forty hours.[6] For the most part, people worked the same hours. "Nine to five," meaning eight hours a day,

Monday through Friday, emerged as the conventional workweek. The term, in addition to conveying the stability that came with work at the time, conveyed that a person was an employee and a subordinate. It began to take on some negative connotations, implying that the work was unfulfilling, the managers autocratic. The 1980 film *9 to 5* highlighted oppressive office life and an uncouth boss—ideas that resonated with many; the film's theme song became Dolly Parton's biggest hit of the decade.

Enlightened companies tried to demonstrate more concern for the well-being of their employees. As companies further embraced paternalism and provided more to address employees' needs, they expected loyalty in return. Harry Levinson, a management expert and family-business psychologist, traced paternalism to ancient clans and kingdoms that needed to sustain their soldiers' loyalty, and says the same approach spread to city-states and eventually became popular in businesses.[7]

What I experienced at IBM was not a unique corporate culture. Many companies at that time, such as Merrill Lynch, EDS, Procter & Gamble, and Price Waterhouse, had similar values: loyalty was paramount. These companies recognized employees for their years of service with paydays, promotions, picnics, and little gold pins.

For many employees, this was welcome. It is always tempting to allow someone else to take care of you. It's more predictable and also preferable to have benefits—and a break. With the paternalistic company, people were comforted by having a safety net. Employees began to count on a company to take care of them, and soon they came to expect it.

There are a lot of people who would welcome the opportunity to work at a paternalistic company. When there's unemployment, many people are thankful for a job, but the problem with

What Defines a Paternalistic Company?

- Loyalty is key.
- Employees put in set hours; "face time" is valued.
- Employees follow a specific employment trajectory based on defined hierarchies.
- Employees stay at the company for a long time, maybe even a lifetime.
- The company is governed by a command-and-control approach.
- Loyalty-based reward systems reign (gold watches instead of company stock).
- The company pays for additional education, but attaches this benefit to longevity constraints. (If you leave, you have to pay them back.)

paternalism is that the dependency it implies introduces a complex conflict. Companies help employees only within the confines of a corporation, not the limitless opportunities of the wider world. This security comes at the cost of the personal growth and independence of the employee. Another issue that both hinders employees and harms companies: when there is a safety net, people don't perform up to their maximum potential. Ultimately everyone is constrained from soaring.

COMPANY FREEFALL

The idea of the paternalistic company that defined previous decades is one that has been propagated and immortalized in pop culture. *Leave It to Beaver* and *The Brady Bunch* depicted the "perfect" family where the wife stayed home and the husband came back at 5:30 PM. Families were able to live off of one income. Families spent time together. They talked around the dinner table.

But in reality, this didn't last long. Family structures and dynamics profoundly changed as social values shifted, divorce rates increased, and more women began to work outside the home. Dual incomes became necessary as property values, the cost of living, and people's expectations all rose.

As society and culture changed at the end of the twentieth century, the role of companies also began to shift. Paternalism became less pronounced as companies couldn't afford to care for their employees at all costs. With increased global competition and need for responsiveness, companies have had to make trade-offs to survive or thrive in this new world. One of the first trade-offs was to give up some of the trappings of the paternalistic company, particularly the notion of lifelong jobs. Whereas corporate jobs once offered security, corporations themselves ceased to be as stable. There were no more job guarantees; there was no such thing as freedom from layoffs.

Pension plans, monthly checks paid upon retirement for the rest of an employee's life, were replaced by defined contribution plans like 401(k)s, which employees paid into and which were first widely adopted in the 1980s as an alternative to the traditional retirement pension. In essence, the 401(k) shifted the burden for retirement savings from the employer to workers.

By 2007, according to the Bureau of Labor Statistics, 33 percent of companies with one hundred workers or more offered a traditional pension (defined benefits) and only 9 percent of firms with fewer than one hundred workers did).[8] In 2009, at least twenty-one large companies announced plans to freeze their pension plans, according to the Pension Rights Center, including Wells Fargo, Cigna, and Anheuser-Busch.[9]

According to the consulting firm Watson Wyatt, some 45 percent of Fortune 100 companies currently offer traditional or hybrid pensions to new hires, down from 49 percent in 2008 and 90 percent in 1998.[10] For many, the safety net for retirement has now ceased to exist.

The once formal recognition of loyalty and dedication has also waned. Whereas receiving a gold pen or special badge for an anniversary of service was once standard operating procedure, and companies like IBM sent employees a silver spoon when a new baby arrived, these practices have been largely eradicated.

Indeed part of this change reflects a new ideal around company longevity. Employee tenure at companies has plummeted. The number of people working more than ten years at one company had declined significantly between 1973 and 2006.[11] At the same time, there is significant "churn"—workers leaving jobs after less than one year—and young people today are far less likely than their parents to have a career characterized by a "lifetime" job with a single employer.[12] In fact, statistics show that the Generation Y (individuals born between 1978 and 2000) employee will have ten jobs by the age of thirty-eight and stay an average of 1.5 years at each job.[13]

In the last decade, paternalism has mostly vanished from many larger companies,[14] and there's a growing mistrust of corporations to take care of you the way your father would. Workers have become angry with the company for letting them down, for changing the dynamic—for abandoning them. But it's not entirely fair to vilify corporate America as deadbeat dads in this way.

It's not as if companies just decided to turn callous and roll back systems that were intended to be good for employees. A lot of companies promote the idea that employees are number one,

How Paternalistic Is Your Company?

- What's the average tenure of employees? More or less than five years?
- Does the company spend more on holiday parties or on training?
- Does it have routine holiday bonuses? Or are bonuses based instead on corporate profits or individual achievements?
- Does the company reward years of service more than contribution? Does it give awards for tenure (service badges, gold pens, seniority-based promotions)? Or are people recognized for directly impacting corporate success, such as generating new customers, creating a new product, or developing areas of expertise within the company?
- Does the company have an egalitarian approach whereby everyone benefits the same regardless of how someone performs, or does it reward top performance?
- When employees leave, are they shunned for not staying loyal to the company, or are they thanked and celebrated?
- How transparent is the culture? Is the company afraid to share org charts or recognition internally or externally because it thinks this information may offend employees or potentially enable recruiters to poach employees, or does it let everyone know when someone is a good performer?

Answers: In each question there are two choices. The first choice describes a paternalistic practice. The second choice describes a culture that is more representative of a meritocracy.

and many of them—eBay, Google, DreamWorks, Southwest, and salesforce.com, to name but a few—do their best to actually model this practice. But in reality, businesses exist to make money and provide returns for investors and shareholders (which we hope also include employees). Businesses function—rightfully so—to provide a return to shareholders, not a free pass for their employees.

All trends point to the fact that the paternalistic company of yesterday is just not as real a possibility in today's world. Companies are simply not in a position to be as loyal to employees as they once were. Companies themselves are no longer in it for the long haul.

The speed at which companies come and go, succeed and fail, is different from even only a short while ago. The half-life of a company is diminishing incredibly quickly. One-third of the companies listed in the 1970 Fortune 500 were gone by 1983. (They were acquired, merged, or split apart.) The average life expectancy of a company in the S&P 500 has dropped from seventy-five years (in 1937) to fifteen years today, according to John Hagel III at Deloitte Center for the Edge.[15]

Simply put, companies don't exist long enough to give you a job for life. We've seen large corporations engage in highly publicized layoffs in response to global competitive pressures. There's something else interesting to recognize here. CYBAEA, a consulting and interim management organization in the United Kingdom, looked at profit-per-employee at 475 of the S&P 500 companies and found that as companies triple the number of employees, productivity drops by half.[16] So the more people companies employ, the less the company gets done? How can that be?

THE NEW MOBILE WORKFORCE

It used to be that you had to move for job opportunities; that's certainly what I did when I was living in Frame 1. Today, however, for the vast majority of employment options, the world has opened up dramatically. The idea of location trumping everything else is now archaic.

REALITY CHECK

The Good and the Bad of Paternalism for Employees and Employers

For employees: "Loyalty" and "family" sound warm and welcoming. Who wouldn't want his or her employer to embrace these values? But it's not that simple. This type of corporate culture also expects employees, like children, to be dependent. It does not empower individuals and doesn't encourage enough independent thinking or self-motivation. When people assume the boss will manage everything, they are deterred from stepping up to new challenges or even adopting a strong solution-oriented outlook. This is limiting because the boss usually offers only the options that are most in line with his or her self-interest or with those of the company, and there are times when those options are directly at odds with the best interest of individuals.

For employers: Paternalism does encourage taking care of employees, which feels good, but it is a dangerous management style. It's expensive to give out routine bonuses that are not tied to performance, and they do not inspire employees to strive for outstanding performance in the same way that "spot" or performance-related bonuses would. Rewarding face time and loyalty as opposed to contribution to business outcomes leads to average performance. Research shows that business health tends to decline and stagnation results from such paternalistic behavior.*

*Craig E. Aronoff and John L. Ward, "The High Cost of Paternalism," *Nation's Business* 81, no. 5 (1993): 61.

Employers must evolve their thinking to understand that they need not be limited to hiring the person closest to headquarters. Companies that want to remain competitive need to hire the best resources, regardless of where they reside. In the future, workers will realize that they can work for the best companies, from wherever they want to live. Horace Greeley's mantra needs to be updated: opportunity is not about going west; it's about being the best.

Of course it's hard to accept this kind of attitude shift when workers are still brainwashed into thinking otherwise. I am always stunned to come across major stories in magazines, newspapers, and blogs about the state of work that allege that work is rooted in certain locations. Each article cites some city or region as the job hotbed du jour. They advocate a move to Lincoln, Nebraska; Fargo, North Dakota; or Sioux Falls, South Dakota—only because they boast jobless rates below 5 percent. That amazes me. If you want to live in Fargo, fantastic, but if you're not a fan, forget about moving there for work.

The trick to finding work outside of Frame 1 is not to look at the Bureau of Labor Statistics monthly metro report and pore over the unemployment rate. The secret is to change how we think about work. It's no longer about accessing the local or cheapest labor source. The Internet's ability to allow the exchange of digital data with anyone, anywhere, and at any time has changed the way we talk to each other, how we access information, how we shop, and how we socialize. It's changed everything, and the next—and perhaps most enduring change—will be in the world of work.

Geoflexibility is going to play a major role in defining the future of work. We now have the tools and technology to work from just about anywhere. Individuals already work 24/7 from home, on vacation, and in coffee shops. Employees will increasingly demand the flexibility to work when and where they want to. The best employees—the best individuals—will thrive working in a meritocracy. Employers that embrace this will be much preferred over traditional companies where face time is more important than outcomes.

LOCATION, LOCATION, LOCATION IS SO YESTERDAY

Something that has always amazed and disappointed me is how we treat humans more poorly than we do our buildings. We treat them as more fungible. Our building leases are for set periods of time, so we can't get out of them; so we lay off our people and keep the buildings. There's always a mismatch in that businesses are continuously looking for talented people, but in tough times they have too many people in aggregate, and in boom times they lose a lot of business opportunity because they don't have the bodies on hand to capture it. I think there's a better way to address this challenge: being less reliant on physical buildings, which will enable a more elastic workforce. This will have an incredible impact on companies. Hiring on-site is rigid, expensive, and time consuming. It takes fifty-two to ninety days to hire someone. Hiring a freelancer is much simpler; for example, online job workplace oDesk has an average hiring timeline of approximately five days—which benefits both companies and workers.

One of the best parts of being at LiveOps is hearing from our independent agents and learning how they leveraged new technology and new thinking to break out of Frame 1. Instead of working as employees, they work as free agents, which allows them to build their careers without sacrificing the other priorities in their lives. These people have seen significant "returns" and have achieved a much better life. Take one independent contractor in Florida who used to race home during the workday to check on her elderly father. As an independent agent, she works from home on her own schedule, allowing her to tend to both work and family needs. Another contractor, a young woman in Philadelphia who dreams of becoming an actress, loves the flexibility that independent contracting provides: it allows her to fit work into her unpredictable audition schedule. And a working mom cherishes being able to see her son when he comes home from school.

These are all simple—but necessary—things, and they are things that work (as we know it) has stolen from us. Who wouldn't want to see their children when they get off the school bus? And yet work schedules often interfere with this very simple joy.

I get incredibly excited because it doesn't have to be this way anymore and because we have so many business cases to demonstrate that it *shouldn't*. We can easily eradicate the tension between work and home lives. We must start to look at them more holistically. It starts with lifting the expectation that we must *go* to work.

Maybe letting go of location, location, location sounds scary, or even impossible. I personally had a hard time giving up some of yesterday's work models, such as having my own office. When I started my career, I used to pride myself on being the first one to arrive at the office and one of the last to leave at night. I loved having an ocean view from my office at Gateway and my own conference room. When I got to eBay, I was floored that I was in an open office, in a cubicle! And the CEO, Meg Whitman, was too!

But what I soon learned by living it was that those old perks—the big office, the fancy furniture, the nice view—were not what made a company effective. They fed our egos, but egos don't grow intellectual capital or revenue or profits. We were wired to think that they would, but they resulted in nothing. On the contrary, not being siloed off in our own offices helped bring democracy and transparency into our organization. We gained access to different levels of management and helped eliminate some outdated and unnecessary hierarchies.

Now the office plan is evolving to a no-office plan, with people increasingly working from home. It makes complete sense, as estimates show that approximately 40 percent of jobs could be performed remotely, at least part of the time. More important, people are looking for something different from work. Almost 80 percent of employees say they would like to work from home at least part of the time, and more than a third say they'd choose the option to work from home over a pay raise.[17] We see across the board that allowing people to work from wherever they want enhances attraction and retention.

Another trend we are seeing is a move away from working for just one employer. Some 80 percent of young people want to be entrepreneurs. High school students are telling pollsters that they never plan on working in a real corporate environment.[18] They want to be CEOs of their own companies. And, having witnessed the collapse of institutions like Bear Stearns, Washington Mutual, and Lehman Brothers (to name just a few), who can blame them? The only safety net they can count on is themselves: their experience, their skills, and their values. Interestingly, research by Deloitte Center for the Edge found that self-employed people are more than twice as likely to be passionate about their work as those who work for firms.[19]

These passionate visionaries who want to do things differently are the individuals who companies need to help them define the future. Companies therefore must figure out a way to harness this shift. Soon they will have no choice.

Some businesses are already enlightened when it comes to the new way of working—and seeing the amazing upside. Real estate is the second-largest expense for most organizations,[20] so determining ways to reduce space results in significant costs savings and competitive advantage. Sun Microsystems, now part of Oracle, recognized how much office space was being wasted and embraced a telework initiative that resulted in more than half of the company's employees working remotely and in a net savings of $80 million a year in facility costs. How so? Flexible work options saved Sun $68 million a year in real estate costs, $3 million a year in reduced power consumption, and $25 million a year in IT expenditures. Sun cofounder Scott McNealy said that the company achieved 10 to 15 percent more activity per employee per week (for those teleworking) versus those who had to come into the office, and that the teleworking employees were happier.[21]

Sun was so pleased with the results it achieved that it spun the initiative into a separate company, Better Workplace, which is bringing these benefits to other companies throughout the world.[22] For example, defense contractor Northrop Grumman worked with Better Workplace to develop Northrop's mobile work strategy and devised a plan to achieve annual savings of $110 million based on 20 percent employee participation. TIAA-CREF, a Fortune 100 financial services organization, used Better Workplace's software tools to manage and scale a flexible work initiative that resulted in the reduction of seventy-five thousand square feet of office space in midtown Manhattan and cost savings of $15 million a year. Though managers were initially concerned about performance issues with employees working remotely, nearly every manager who participated in a survey responded that employees performed as well—or better—when working from home. In another example, ATB Financial, a full-service financial institution headquartered in Edmonton, Alberta, Canada, which was named one of Canada's 50 Best Employers by *Report on Business* magazine and one of the 75 Best Workplaces in Canada by the Great Place to Work Institute, wanted to explore a more flexible work initiative to remain competitive and maintain its stance as a great employer. Through a pilot program, it discovered it could reduce office space by eighty-eight thousand square feet and save approximately $2.6 million annually. It also found that each employee who participated in the program could save approximately one week a year in commute time!

At LiveOps, we see the advantages our customers gain with flexibility and elasticity: ProFlowers enlists our agents during high traffic times such as Mother's Day or Valentine's Day, and benefits from having an on-demand workforce that it can ramp up or down.

The advantages of a more flexible workforce are evident: lower overhead for the company, broader access to talent, and greater elasticity in getting work done efficiently. Traditional work is becoming increasingly flexible in accommodating the new work paradigm. That makes sense. Consider that the Telework Research Network found that having employees work from home half of the time could save employers over $10,000 per employee per year as a result of increased productivity, reduced facility costs, lowered absenteeism, and reduced turnover.[23]

Enlightened companies see the world of work differently: there is a global economy consisting of suppliers and buyers of talent. In many ways it's the eBay way. Just as eBay revolutionized the world of e-commerce (and eradicated the sole reliance on stores, set prices, and shopping for items only within driving distance), we can now tap into this same idea to revolutionize the world of work. There are new ways to get work done, which eliminate the dependency on office buildings, commuting, and set work hours day in and day out.

Jobs will come back when the economy recovers, but they will never be the same. My kids will never have to move for a job the way I did. They won't have to go to an office every day—something I had to do through much of my career, and something that denied me living near members of my family.

Much as I realized that IBM would not take care of me in the paternalistic way I once believed it would, and realized that I am the only one who can take care of me and my career, you too have probably recognized that you are the only one who can take care of your career. But we need to go a step beyond this. We need you not only to take charge of your own destiny but also to take charge of changing work. We can't wait for CEOs to change it for us (even if it makes sense for them to do so); we must be the ones to spur change in the world of work.

5

Frame 2: CEO of Your Own Destiny

Rebecca Graf didn't want to admit it, but the way she was working simply wasn't working. On paper, things looked perfect. An accountant for twenty years, Rebecca had a good job working in the finance department at a pharmaceutical manufacturing company in Milwaukee, Wisconsin. She made a nice salary and received a raise of at least 7 percent every year, and she always got a bonus. There were also attractive benefits, including health insurance and a 401(k) plan, which helped her feel secure.

But while the job kept her family's finances relatively in order, the rest of Rebecca's life was in disarray. Married with three school-age children, she had tried a variety of child-care options over the years: an aunt watched her kids at one point; later they went to a public day care, and they eventually enrolled in private day care at a school where Rebecca's husband, Travis, worked. She never saw her kids leave in the morning, and she wasn't there when they came home in the afternoon. She missed all of the parent-teacher conferences and never went on field trips. "I felt like I wasn't a part of my family," Rebecca says. She also admits that her house was a constant mess, which stressed her out further.

Rebecca worked the hours her company demanded, which meant until 1 or 2 AM when it was time to close the books each month. Although she regularly started work at 5 or 6 AM, two hours before her boss arrived, she got reprimanded for leaving fifteen minutes early for medical appointments, although she had been granted permission to do so. Her boss said her early hours didn't count if no one was there to see them.

This was the corporate culture, which Rebecca describes as "harsh and demanding." "They wanted to follow everything by the book, even if it didn't follow common sense," she says. Although there were only two hundred people on-site, the company was owned by a global conglomerate, and the division followed the larger company's rules. Although this location didn't contract with the government or do any highly secure or confidential work, only employees were allowed past the lobby. Rebecca's husband couldn't go to the cafeteria to join her for lunch, and her six-year old daughter couldn't visit her office when her family picked Rebecca up at the end of the day. Management wasn't sympathetic when one of her children was home sick. When she asked for two days off to attend her father's funeral, her boss stressed his concern about how to classify her absence on the attendance sheet—before he offered his condolences.

Rebecca wanted more control over her life, but she felt trapped by the security of a salary and benefits. She also felt that she was obliged to keep her job and be grateful to have it. Her father, who was born in the late 1920s, only changed jobs when he became too elderly to do physically demanding work. Growing up with that as a model, Rebecca believed that you stayed in the same job until "you got the gold watch." Rebecca was trapped in Frame 1.

Then one morning Rebecca had an epiphany when her boss told her that as his daughter waved good-bye at the window, he realized he hadn't seen his little girl in a week. At that moment, she realized that when she died, the company wouldn't care, but her family would. She discussed her desire to find a more flexible job with her husband, who supported her decision, and soon after handed in her notice.

She took a job as a financial analyst at the American Society for Quality, a nonprofit network of institutions and organizations across various industries that provides education and certifications. The job offered her flexibility, and she was able to work from home when family circumstances, such as a sick child, required her to do so. Then Rebecca's husband got transferred for work, and she telecommuted for a year until the demands of the job required that she be in the office every week. Her company put her in nice hotels and paid for her meals, but she wasn't seeing her kids, which took too great a toll. She negotiated a new package in which she would give up being an employee but continue working as a consultant. The new role would allow her to telecommute and work her own hours. She would have to sacrifice her benefits, but it was worth it. "I took control and got to work on my own terms."

Rebecca enjoyed the arrangement for a little more than a year and even saw an increase in salary when she was paid for her time, but by 2009 the organization began to face financial difficulty, and she was let go. That change was not as jarring as it would have been had she still been an employee with an always consistent income stream and benefits. Already accustomed to being paid for her time and setting her own hours, she transitioned into the world of freelancing fairly seamlessly.

She found a freelance job as a virtual assistant, and although she did not make as much money as she had before, she still had the ability to work from home and set her own hours, enabling her to attend her daughter's volleyball games and chaperone her son's field trips. Part of her job included writing articles and testing out blog platforms. She fell in love with the work. When the family moved to South Dakota for her husband's new job teaching history and English at a public high school, Rebecca was able to continue working the same job. She even pursued her dream of going back to school to become a teacher as well, enrolling in online classes. She's found her true passion in writing and has found the time and drive to write a book, a romance mystery novel. She's also collaborated with friends to start her own publishing company, Silver Tongue Press, which publishes other writers' works. "We are living our dreams now," she says.

Rebecca admits that money is tighter than before, but whenever she starts to worry, a new writing assignment comes in, and she says that her income is starting to increase. She's structured her schedule so that she can spend more time with her family, and she saves the biggest paychecks to splurge on road trips. "I can go on a family vacation or go stay at my mom's house for a few weeks and help her," Rebecca says of her newfound flexibility. "With an Internet connection, I can work whenever from wherever I want."

She also says she's exponentially happier living in Frame 2. "I'm so close to achieving what I want to do," she says. "I'm loving every minute of it."

————————

The Framework: Where Do You See Yourself?

Paternalistic Era	The Age of Entrepreneurship
Frame 1	**Frame 2**
Company Man or Woman	**CEO of Your Own Destiny**
• You are a high achiever.	• You are highly successful.
• You have a great attitude.	• You are self-aware.
• You are on a promotion track.	• You love the freedom this choice has given you.
• You have only as much future as the company you are with.	• You opt in to being fully on the team every day.
	• You work to build a network outside the office "walls."
	• You have great and fulfilling career options.
Recommendation: *Continue your emphasis on high performance, but broaden your view of your career beyond the constraints of any one company.*	**Recommendation:** *You can work for yourself or a corporation and still be the CEO of Your Own Destiny. This is the sweet spot for the future of work.*
Frame 3	**Frame 4**
Disenchanted Employee	**Aspiring Entrepreneur**
• You are waiting to be discovered or recognized.	• You fully embrace controlling your own destiny.
• You can't understand why others don't understand how good you are.	• You don't have enough work to do on the terms you are willing to do it.
• You are not progressing in your career at the speed you expected.	• You may not be addressing the gaps between your desires and your skills.
• You believe your circumstances to be someone else's problem.	
Recommendation: *Take a meaningful look at what you want to achieve and the steps you will take to achieve it.*	**Recommendation:** *Reassess your value proposition to understand why your view of your value is not aligned with your current environment; make appropriate course corrections.*

Meritocracy: feels personally invested, proactive, positive, willing

Entitlement: feels deserving, frustrated, critical

There are millions of hardworking people who, like Rebecca Graf, have found that corporate careers just don't cut it for them any longer. This sentiment has only grown in a persistent down economy, as many companies no longer offer the same security or incentives they once did, with salaries flat and health care and other benefits scaled back. (In other words, the great job with the 7 percent raise Rebecca received in 2004 often doesn't even exist today.) Concurrent with this reality, today's most inspired and achievement-oriented employees spurn the idea of "golden handcuffs" and yearn for more choices in this complex world. Some employees just don't think that the constraints of corporate jobs—showing up on a certain schedule at a certain location—are worth the personal sacrifices. For others, there's nothing like the freedom, excitement, and the flexibility of working for themselves. Studies have shown that workers are more than twice as likely to be passionate when self-employed.[1]

It sounds liberating to live in Frame 2. It sounds empowering. It sounds different. Maybe it even sounds impossible. Amazingly, however, becoming the CEO of Your Own Destiny is neither a new idea nor a novel approach. In fact, for most of history, individuals worked for themselves. For most of history, people have been in charge of their careers—and their lives.

Prior to the Civil War, most Americans worked in agriculture or as small merchants and tradesmen.[2] Success was the result of self-direction, self-motivation, and self-determination. In a way, everyone was self-made.

The Industrial Revolution brought opportunities to work outside the home, reversing the entrepreneurial spirit and giving rise to the paternalistic company, but now the Age of Entrepreneurship is bringing it back.

As companies have tried (and failed) to keep up with global competitiveness and corporate culture has changed, so too has the psyche of employees. Work-life balance became a topic of hot debate, and people began to express their disenchantment with work. The modern workforce evolved into one that is striking back at the company: it longs for freedom and feels shackled by the old methods. Generation X, the forty-six million born between 1965 and 1978 and the ones primed as today's leaders, are massively disenchanted with work. They report that they are working more than ever, with 31 percent of high-earning Xers having an "extreme job" and 28 percent working an average of ten hours more per week than three years ago, according to research by the Center for Work-Life Policy (CWLP, now known as the Center for Talent Innovation).[3] They report serious repercussions for their health and family relationships. The CWLP study finds that with "little chance of fulfilling their career ambitions or being rewarded for their efforts, 37% have 'one foot out the door' and are looking to leave their current employers in the next three years."

Frame 2 is the sweet spot for work because people who operate with a Frame 2 mind-set know that they are in charge of their destiny. They fully embrace and accept the accountability for this and thus are far more likely to actually achieve their dreams.

There are people like Rebecca who fully live in Frame 2 and embrace being the CEO of their own destiny so completely that they can't stand the idea of working for anybody else ever again. I see this a lot in the entrepreneurs whom I fund in the start-up world. However, this represents only a small portion of the population. There are far more people who want to live with a Frame 2 mind-set—they want to be in control—but who, for myriad reasons, are unwilling to deal with the risk of starting their own business or working entirely on their own as an independent contractor. There are headaches they want to avoid, such as the responsibilities of health care payments, funding their own retirement accounts, and having to do everything from marketing to IT to billing and collections. Many people simply enjoy the camaraderie and collaboration that a corporate environment can provide.

There is nothing wrong with this, and many people can be very successful at keeping a Frame 2 mind-set but still work for an organization. Most of the top executives with whom I have interacted actually operate with a Frame 2 point of view, although they have worked most of their careers in companies. This is actually where I spent the majority of my career once I left IBM; I was a successful executive who enjoyed working for companies, but who understood that I was accountable for how far I would go in my career.

Companies are consistently looking to hire the best and the brightest talent. Hiring somebody who lives in Frame 2—who understands the importance of personal responsibility and is passionate about his or her career—is an excellent way to get great talent. Frame 2 people will be more likely to jump at other opportunities if they are not challenged and growing at their current companies; it is therefore in companies' best interests to continuously hone their effectiveness at ensuring that their top talent continues to learn and to be constantly challenged.

I am always amazed about how excited we are, both from a company and an employee perspective, on day one of a new job. The employee is, one hopes, a very talented person who had lots of opportunities and decided to select employment at this particular organization. The company, one hopes, had lots of talented people who wanted the opening, and it chose the new employee for the open slot because he or she was the best. In other words, everyone was voted on to the team. Everyone is happy. Unfortunately, however, all too often, this energy quickly dissipates. The talented employee comes to feel that this is just a job, and the employer starts thinking that the employee is lucky to have a job and be there.

The truth of the situation is that talented employees always have lots of options for where to work and that companies that want to keep talented workers will only do so by being the place that these employees can learn the most, accomplish the most, and enjoy the most. There are tough problems in every company, but when employees are cherished and challenged and they know the company has their back, they will do amazing things. Employees who join companies and don't do a stellar job are in danger of failing to fulfill their career aspirations and in even more danger of actually losing their job. Adopting a Frame 2 mind-set will help individuals feel a stronger sense of purpose and make them more successful, whether they work for themselves within an organization or entirely on their own.

More people are creating new ways to make living in Frame 2 a reality, and in doing so, defining a new way for everyone to work. Take, for instance, Campbell McKellar, a young woman I met though my investment network. Campbell had always been an entrepreneur. She started her first business, a photography company, when she was at Princeton, and later launched a non-profit that provided consulting services to other nonprofits. But by the time she graduated from college and earned her MBA from Stanford, she had a pile of student debt. She took a corporate job at Goldman Sachs to help pay it off.

Campbell was the archetypal Company Woman. Entrenched fully in Frame 1, she describes the Goldman job as "gold plated."

She explains, "They paid for my dinner every night. A black car took me home." However, she was well aware of the costs. A nice lifestyle didn't result in a nice life. She worked from 5 AM until 7 PM, seven days a week. "Some people thrive on that. That was so *not* me," she says.

Wanting more mobility and freedom, Campbell took a job at a commercial real estate company where she could work from wherever she wanted. She did, completing assignments from Guatemala and northern Maine. That experience brought her an entrepreneurial epiphany: she realized that she could do her job remotely—and a number of her friends probably could too—but sometimes, she also wanted a defined and productive place to work. Thinking about all the workplaces with empty desks and spaces that could be rented out, she created Loosecubes as a community marketplace to connect open work space with people who need it. Similar to Zipcar, Loosecubes brings a communal time-share model to work. The benefits of sharing a work space with other professionals are more than economic; these people gain the additional benefit of sharing space with potential new collaborators, clients, and contacts. This "coworking" opportunity, which enables a benefit of "cross-pollination," has even caught the attention of bigger employers. Nearly 10 percent of U.S. coworking users in 2011 were employed at companies with more than one hundred people, according to Emergent Research and the coworking site Deskmag.[4]

Campbell says that since switching to a remote-work model, she works the same number of hours as when she was at Goldman Sachs, but she does it differently. Dictating her own hours, she comes into the office after 10:30 AM, preferring to exercise before work and stay later in the evenings. Similarly, Loosecubes' members, a combination of mobile workers, remote employees,

Workplaces in the Cloud

The following sites connect talent to jobs:

CrowdFlower: a platform that takes large, information-heavy projects and breaks them into small tasks that can be distributed to on-demand contributors worldwide.

Elance: a platform for online employment, connecting talented individuals to businesses looking to staff-up a team on an hourly or project basis.

Guru: a marketplace for online talent that allows businesses to find, hire, and manage freelancers.

LiveOps: a cloud-based contact or call center that has a community of twenty thousand independent agents who work from wherever they want, whenever they want, and handle more than seventy million customer interactions per year.

oDesk: an online workplace that enables businesses to select professionals based on work history, portfolio, feedback ratings and reviews, and test scores.

Samasource: a virtual work marketplace comprising thousands of women and youth who live in refugee camps in Haiti, Kenya, and other countries. The company has set up digital work tents with high-speed Internet connectivity, where people perform computer-based work (such as content review) on behalf of Silicon Valley technology companies.

entrepreneurs, and business travelers, also work in untraditional ways. She says they share common values, looking for "more out of work and life." Many of Loosecubes' clients are not pursuing one job but instead are doing multiple things and doing them at all sorts of hours, evidenced by the demand to rent work space on the weekends and in the evenings.

"The way work has changed: you no longer have a company, a title, and a role," she says. "People are weaving work and life together at times that work best for their lives." Campbell built her business on the premise that workplaces should be people-centric rather than company-centric, something she believes defines business as we know it. "Work has changed," she says. "The office needs to catch up."

Campbell is right, but instead of waiting for the office or the employer to "catch up," everyone must be empowered to ignite his or her own change. What do you want to do? Your change need not be as grandiose as quitting a high-paying job to starting your own business. Perhaps your dream is to make as much money as you do now and still be able to pick your kids up from school. Or maybe it's to cut down your commute and work

Why Freelancers Freelance

According to a survey of contractors by online job workplace oDesk,*

- 87 percent of contractors said that they want to be self-employed.
- 74 percent of contractors said that they preferred an online workplace to an on-site workplace.

Reasons cited for preferring online work:

- 92 percent said that making money is important.
- 89 percent cited flexible hours.
- 83 percent wanted to be able to work wherever.
- 63 percent wanted to be able to find more interesting work.

*oDesk's survey results were based on 8,472 responses from the online workplace's active contractors, who tend to be well-educated early adopters and innovators of technology.

more flexible hours. Maybe you want to stay at your current job, but work from home one day a week. We live in an era in which all of these options are possible.

EVERYONE HAS TO GET VOTED ON TO THE TEAM EVERY DAY

We have so many myths about work. As we've already discussed, most of us go to work; we put in set hours Monday through Friday; we get defined vacation time and sick days each year; we work for one or a few companies. Many employers are starting to see through these myths, which helps bring this revolution—and the attainment of Frame 2 status for everyone—closer to reality.

The trend toward adopting flex work is under way and gaining momentum. Flexibility is important to today's workforce; in fact, it's the most important factor. That's what we found at LiveOps. According to a survey of LiveOps' independent agent community, 66 percent of respondents cited work flexibility as the *number-one* reason they have chosen to contract with LiveOps. Zappos, which has paved the way in customer satisfaction, has also become a model for employee satisfaction by providing each customer service rep with a degree of choice and autonomy that far exceeds levels of flexibility at other contact centers.

The model is very different from the one that most generations grew up with, which measured work ethic by physical presence (face time). Although this new metric is immediately liberating, it is the individual's long-term responsibility to understand it. You have to be aware of trends and what's hot and determine for yourself where you'll be relevant. Companies won't do this for you. The new world of work is about accepting responsibility and taking initiative.

In the old paradigm, workers might have felt safe, but work was not as fulfilling, and there was little opportunity to make choices. This security was a way to manage risk, but not a way to achieve one's destiny. There's a danger that comes with complacency. Workers do not strive to be their best. Furthermore, managers don't demand it. They manage to the average—not to the excellent. It's time for all of us to demand more.

The opportunity to push these ideas forward and into the future is exciting. We are only at the beginning of the changes in work. The next ten years will bring even more profound ones as technology continues to advance to become faster, better, and easier to use, as well as even cheaper, making it accessible to everyone. The importance of location will continue to dissipate in the wireless, hyperconnected, global world. With this freedom will come reduced dependence on a company; in fact, the employee-employer relationship will eventually cease to exist. Individuals will become their own employers, deciding what kind of work to accept and working on many projects or for several entities at the same time.

Work is dramatically different from where it was fifty years ago—and from where it will be in the future.

Through the Years: The Changing World of Work

1960	2013	2020
Work locally	Work from anywhere	Hyperconnected; global orientation
Job for life	Ten to fourteen jobs by age thirty-eight	Wired, seamless, in constant search-and-find mode
9 to 5	24/7 (if you like)	Collaborative
Single income	Dual income	Many income streams
Work and home are separate	Work at home	Immediate, on-demand access

This is the future of work. When individuals recognize the fundamentals of Frame 2—that they are in charge and must stop ceding control to a boss or looking externally to an employer for security—they will open up entirely new possibilities in which they can decide what to work on, when to work on it, and where they want to work.

When you live in Frame 2, you experience an interesting mix of total freedom and total accountability. It is fantastic to completely control what you want to spend time on and with whom, every day. However, Frame 2 also requires you to be relevant every day and to be voted on to the team you want to play with. With unparalleled degrees of freedom comes unparalleled accountability. It's invigorating and scary at the same time, but real entrepreneurs wouldn't want it any other way.

In the spirit of providing mentoring and guidance, I've developed a worksheet that can help you on the way to becoming the CEO of Your Own Destiny. The questions and concepts below are designed to help you build a credible and achievable path to your dreams. An extended version of this worksheet for you to fill out, as well as sample worksheets that I've completed at various inflection points in my career, are also included in the appendices.

Becoming the CEO of Your Own Destiny

1. Aim High

Project yourself five years into the future. You are in a room on stage. Tell your audience where you are in your life. What has your audience in awe? What would you view as wild success?

If you hear "I can't" when you try to think about your dreams, write down the impediments that you see.

Realize how much is holding you back. Now, consciously let it go.

Start again. Think about what you want. Dream big. Think about your personal and professional lives synergistically. These are not separate dreams. What is your potential, your life purpose? What does success look like to you?

Now, what does success look like in nine months?

In two years?

In five years?

Note: This Aim High step is not easy. If truly done well, this will take some energy and soul searching. When you take time to really ponder what you want to do, it is very likely to be hard and even uncomfortable. That's okay.

If you are having difficulty articulating clearly what your "Aim High" goals are, stop and answer the following questions.

- Does combining personal and career goals cause the problem? If so, do the worksheet separately for each and then do the consolidated one.
- Can you articulate Aim High goals in your personal life? If not, think about the things that are holding you back from being able to articulate the goals. Write them down. If your goals are still unclear, you may need to seek some outside coaching or counseling. Dedicating time to talk about these issues will help bring some of the answers to light.
- Can you articulate Aim High goals in your professional life? If not, what questions come into your head that prevent you from achieving clarity? List the questions individually and write down the answers to the best of your ability. If your goals are still unclear, you may need to seek help from a mentor.

The most important aspect of the Aim High exercise is to be totally honest about what you want to achieve. Don't get intimidated by the sacrifices required to achieve your ultimate potential. This section of the worksheet is about your aspirations, not your impediments. (We'll worry about those later.)

2. The Spirit of "And"

What matters most to you in your life? Life is not about pursuing a single purpose. We all have many roles and we've compartmentalized our work and home lives. People have looked at these as separate spheres. I encourage you to look at them holistically. Here's what most people don't understand: these dual roles do not have to compete. They can co-exist and work together, even complement one another. Achieving this, however, requires some planning. You can't have it all with a haphazard approach.

List the different successes that you want to achieve. Be specific. Some examples: ensuring that you are fully available for your children; providing for their college education; being a fully present partner or spouse; achieving economic freedom; having a successful and fulfilling career. The trick here is to recognize what is most important. Prioritize the list.

I want you to dream big, and with the advances we talked about you can achieve more than ever, but you still need to determine what matters most to you. Even if you've embraced the spirit of "AND", AND you want to do it all, you must recognize that you can't always achieve everything. You must make decisions to determine what's most important so that you can ultimately achieve your goals.

You must always ask the hard question: What trumps what?

3. How Can I?

Are there examples, role models, and resources available that illuminate how to achieve your goals? Who else is doing what you want to be doing? What can you learn from them?

List the people you are inspired by who can serve as role models. (You do not have to know them personally.)

Determine how you will figure out their secrets to success or whatever it is you admire most about them. What will you read about them? Is it possible to engage with them?

Given what you've learned, what have you determined your path should be?

4. Do What You Say, Say What You Do

Southwest Airlines CEO *Herb Kelleher* once said, "We have a strategic plan . . . It's called doing things." It's time to do things. It's time to commit to an action plan—one that you can follow.

List three to five things in each of the following categories:

What will you START doing (that is new and different)?

What will you STOP doing (that is holding you back from your dreams of success)?

What will you CONTINUE doing (that you want to take with you on your journey)?

5. Step Back and Reflect

Now that you have gone through this process and have some perspective, go back and think about your Aim High goals. Do they still resonate with you? Has anything changed?

Success builds on success, so checking in frequently on the goals and readjusting them as you progress is important.

6

Frame 3: The Disenchanted Employee

I remember receiving some early coaching advice from an MIT professor. He told his seminar class a story about taking his daughter crabbing in the Boston Bay. She was very worried about there being no lid on the pail. The professor told his daughter that no lid was needed—anytime one of the crabs started working its way to the top, another would reach up and pull it down. The moral of the story was that chronically negative people (crabs) would bring the whole team down and never allow any one of them or the team to reach new heights.

I often ask managers how many of their team they would rehire if they were starting over. In my entire career, there is only one time that a manager told me that he would rehire everyone on his team. We actually should be striving to have a team full of high-potential, high-performing individuals. If you have a couple of Frame 3 employees on your team, I assure you that your entire team will suffer.

If you live in Frame 3, please look hard at yourself in the mirror and realize that it's time to take the steps needed to get to another frame. I find that people who live chronically in Frame 3 tend to have a detrimental, negative outlook—and with it come significant ramifications: other people will be far less interested in spending additional time with them, offering them additional opportunities, or cheering them on. Any other frame is better than Frame 3 — and a step closer to Frame 2, where we should all want to be.

The Framework: Where Do You See Yourself?

	Paternalistic Era	**The Age of Entrepreneurship**
Meritocracy: feels personally invested, proactive, positive, willing	**Frame 1** **Company Man or Woman** • You are a high achiever. • You have a great attitude. • You are on a promotion track. • You have only as much future as the company you are with. **Recommendation:** *Continue your emphasis on high performance, but broaden your view of your career beyond the constraints of any one company.*	**Frame 2** **CEO of Your Own Destiny** • You are highly successful. • You are self-aware. • You love the freedom this choice has given you. • You opt in to being fully on the team every day. • You work to build a network outside the office "walls." • You have great and fulfilling career options. **Recommendation:** *You can work for yourself or a corporation and still be the CEO of Your Own Destiny. This is the sweet spot for the future of work.*
Entitlement: feels deserving, frustrated, critical	**Frame 3** **Disenchanted Employee** • You are waiting to be discovered or recognized. • You can't understand why others don't understand how good you are. • You are not progressing in your career at the speed you expected. • You believe your circumstances to be someone else's problem. **Recommendation:** *Take a meaningful look at what you want to achieve and the steps you will take to achieve it.*	**Frame 4** **Aspiring Entrepreneur** • You fully embrace controlling your own destiny. • You don't have enough work to do on the terms you are willing to do it. • You may not be addressing the gaps between your desires and your skills. **Recommendation:** *Reassess your value proposition to understand why your view of your value is not aligned with your current environment; make appropriate course corrections.*

WORK REALLY COULD BE KILLING YOU

On-the-job stress is cited as the number-one reason for employee dissatisfaction in the American workforce: 40 percent of Americans say their job is "very or extremely stressful"; one in four employees view it as the number-one stressor in their lives; 42 percent say the stress interferes with their family or personal lives.[1] The prime causes of all this stress, according to a Harris Interactive poll, are low pay, commuting, unreasonable workload, and fear of being fired or laid off.[2]

The statistics are alarming—this type of stress and unhappiness leads to Frame 3—the worst place for employees to be. I really worry about people who spend the majority of their time in this space. It's unhealthy for companies and for individuals.

Studies have found that unhappiness at work has a significant negative impact on one's health. Unlike one hundred years ago, when work was physically dangerous, in this century, work has become more psychologically dangerous. Sound crazy? Not really: research shows that chronic levels of work stress increase the risk of everything from the common cold to Alzheimer's, heart disease, and depression. In fact, numerous studies have found that "psychosocial" factors—like work-related stress—represent the single most important variable in determining how long somebody lives.[3]

Here's the amazing thing about what causes the most stress in our modern world. What stresses people out the most is not the number of hours in the workday or the bad nature of their boss, but the feeling that they have little say over their day. People are most unhappy when they can't choose their own projects or make their own decisions about what to focus on first.[4] Therefore, folks in Frame 3—those who feel least in control and most like a victim of their fate—are the most at risk.

It's an unfortunate state of affairs that people are so unhappy at work, especially when Americans spend so much of their lifetimes in the office. This is especially disheartening when we consider how easy it is to change. People who are living in Frame 2, those who feel that they are the CEOs of their own destinies and calling their career shots, are happier. A Gallup poll found that self-employed people in the United States are the happiest workers and work the hardest[5] because they have a "higher measure of self-determination and freedom."[6] Furthermore, this free choice, or being "the boss of you," was a bigger predictor of happiness than making more money or achieving a greater sense of democracy and social tolerance.[7] Need further evidence? The research of Italian economist Paolo Verme found that freedom and control are by far the most significant predictors of life satisfaction anywhere in the world.[8] They come before money, demonstrating that pursuing what you want is a lot more rewarding than pursuing a paycheck.

That's why we see that home-based workers are sick or absent less often than people who work in an office. Not only does work make some people sick, but there is a whole population of people who fake an illness to shirk work. Consider that 78 percent of employees who call in sick aren't really sick.[9] These individuals are stuck in Frame 3, unhappy with their jobs and cranky about it, but not doing anything meaningful to change it. And Frame 3 is certainly costly to companies: these unscheduled absences cost employers $1,800 per employee per year—totaling $300 billion per year for U.S. companies.[10] Employers could stop this waste and use the savings toward other functions that produce a return, such as investing in innovation.

Living in Frame 3 isn't sustainable. Luckily, there's a clear path out: understanding how you got here; taking the time to

When You Find Yourself in Frame 3

- Accept that you are in an unproductive place.
- Own that it is your responsibility to get to a better place.
- Understand the issues or perceptions, either real or imagined, that led to your living in Frame 3.
- Assess the reality of the situation:
- How much positive support do you have among your peers, managers, and upper management? (Would they rehire you now that they know the kind of work you do?)
- If there is damage, is it recoverable?
- Do everything possible to remedy the situation (as Stephen Covey put it, seek first to understand, and then to be understood), either in this situation or in the next job.
- Commit to doing and perceiving things differently, then follow up on that commitment.
- Find a way to give heartfelt praise to coworkers when something is well done.

think about what you really want; creating a plan, as discussed in Chapter Five; and working with a few trusted mentors and advisers, as we'll discuss in the next section.

THE MENTOR MANDATE

Whether you are a winning gymnast in the Olympics, a tennis player in the U.S. Open, or a pitcher in the major leagues, you got to the pinnacle of your career with a mix of natural ability, hard work, and coaching. We understand that in sports there is a great coach behind every great player, and we celebrate these folks, but in work we somehow forget their importance. We leave behind what we learned in school athletics and approach our professional lives without giving much thought to coaching (mentoring) or where to look to continue to build our skills and abilities and be the best we can be.

That's a mistake. Everyone does better with someone watching. All of us can benefit from a mentor who can observe, offer insight, and guide us. Atul Gawande, a successful surgeon, asked a former teacher to serve as his mentor, even though Gawande was well established in his career. It was an untraditional move, and one that unnerved some of his patients, but Gawande felt that the relationship made him better in his craft—helped him understand things he might have missed because he was set in his way of doing things. He compared the experience of this kind of coaching in medicine to the way professional musicians have coaches, whom they refer to as "outside ears." He wanted to bring that perspective into his profession—and into others, to anyone who "just want[s] to do what they do as well as they can."[11]

I owe much of my personal and professional success to mentors. As it did for most people, this guidance came in its earliest form from my athletics coaches. Charlie Rowe in Little League and Abner Bigbie in high school football helped me find my talents and hone my skills. Cognizant that I had lost my dad, they stepped in and served as role models and inspiring coaches both on and off the field. Later, I found mentors at work. At IBM, one of my mentors, John Martone (a guy with a wood desk, signifying that he'd made it), suggested I start dressing more professionally, and then helped me do so by giving me some of his old suits. He told me to walk with purpose (as though I knew where I was going), and he helped me crisp up my writing.

Even though I was, for much of my career, a company guy, I consistently looked for inspiration outside the walls of my organization. Perhaps I did that because I understood the influence of my coaches in my youth, but most of all because I needed to. When I left IBM, I worked for much smaller companies that didn't have nearly the same focus on people that IBM did. There were no formal programs offered, so I had to develop mentors and coaches on my own. Furthermore, as my career progressed, I found that the right kind of mentors and role models I needed to help me grow did not exist within my company.

In 1992, I was an IT network director (working on how computers and people interact with each other) when I decided I wanted to become a chief information officer (CIO). It was a very cool emerging new job that would put me in charge of the internal systems and infrastructure processes that companies use to operate all of their business and interact with customers and suppliers. It was a challenging job no one wanted; it required completing multimillion-dollar projects on time and converting tech talk to business speak. There wasn't a handbook on how to do this, particularly as the role evolved in the late 1980s and early 1990s. (It was during this time that tech professionals were first elevated to the executive suite.) I wanted to be a part of this growing field and was especially excited about the next wave that incorporated information technology into business strategy.

Not knowing whom to tap for advice at my own company, I took matters into my own hands. I subscribed to CIO magazines and created a database of people I admired. I read studies and discovered the thought leaders in the burgeoning space. I went to industry events and listened to luminaries in my field. I got to know who they were, what they were about, and, most important, what success looked like to them.

I created a "CIO List" from the database I developed. I tracked who they were, how I knew them, and their remarkable accomplishments. I urge you to do this, but please be mindful of people's time and respectful of their boundaries. Remember that creating relationships with your role models can be about giving more than getting. I didn't want to meet these individuals for their fame; I wanted to learn how they achieved and sustained their success so that I could become better at my trade and ultimately make a better contribution to this space. Today, making these kinds of connections is easier than ever, as so much of this valuable information is available on the Web. Yahoo! and Google made it possible to search anything. Nearly everyone has a LinkedIn profile that highlights his or her career path. Industry leaders write articles and position papers and blogs. Read them.

With office buildings and hierarchies on the wane, workers have to go out and build connections themselves. I urge you to see the importance of mentors, but untangle them from the workplace. Like everything else in the changing world of work, these pivotal relationships will not develop in the office. They will come from your network. This is good news and a serious upgrade: the network has more power and influence than does one assigned mentor. With a network culled from a variety of areas, you gain access to the best and brightest minds that have the most experience specifically relevant to you and your dreams.

Once upon a time, mentors and coaches were assigned to employees. Workers were given a very clear road map to follow, and the definitions of success were clear (even if some of them were crazy). This kind of defined structure scarcely exists anymore, for a few reasons. Employee tenure has consistently become shorter, which makes getting advice or help from one's company less practical than ever. In addition, middle management has been slashed, and there are fewer folks with enough bandwidth to help. Competition is fierce, and in some cases, people worry about

Nurture Your Network

- *Find the best mentors?*

  Who does your current job—or the job you want—well? Read industry publications and websites and blogs to identify the best people in your field. Search Google. Find them on LinkedIn. Connect with them on a mentoring matching service. What is their magic? Create a database of who they are, what they've accomplished, and what you can learn from them.

- *Seek advice from the best people. (Don't be shy. Reach out.)*

  People love to mentor, help, and coach. Ask your mentors what success looks like to them. Ask them what they think has made them successful. Ask them to share their story. (People love talking about themselves.)

- *Bring value to the network.*

  Ask what you can do to help your mentors. You may have assets they need. Don't be a pest, but do send a relevant article or a post they might find interesting, or promote their work to your network. Social media tools make this easier than ever.

- *Ask questions.*

  This will give you the best education.

training their own replacement, someone the company may view as newer and less expensive. With people concerned about making themselves redundant, there's no longer an opportunity to receive years of coaching from one boss. This shift away from internal coaching is only going to be exacerbated by further shrinkages in employee tenure, and location will matter less as more people work remotely and become more entrepreneurial (either starting their own companies or becoming freelancers). Also, mentoring seldom exists at underresourced, fast-paced start-ups.

Where does this leave us? Jim Billington presciently wrote in 1997 that "the traditional mentor-protégé relationship has gone the way of the mainframe computer—while it hasn't completely disappeared, it isn't nearly as common as it used to be. Reengineering, flatter organizations, and a lack of gray-haired senior vice presidents have all contributed to the decline."[12] Now, more than fifteen years later, in the age of iPad and tablets, the mainframe has disappeared, and the mentor-protégé relationship has gone with it.

We have to acknowledge that in the Age of Entrepreneurship, the onus of personal and professional development is on the individual, not on the company. I hope that instead of fearing this new responsibility, you'll see the many benefits it brings. One of the most crucial improvements is that it eradicates the inherent conflict of interest that comes from getting advice from your employer. There are very few mentors within your company who are actively committed to having you consider extending your career outside of their company (especially if you are a star performer). You can understand why: there are never enough of the best resources on hand, and it would take a very selfless leader to be willing to lose a great talent.

Just think of how upset companies get when others (particularly competitors) recruit their best people. They call it poaching—clearly looking at it through a lens that focuses on the loss to the company, not the possible personal gain and benefit to the employee. (This is not an approach that benefits individuals. Professor Matt Marx at MIT's Sloan School of Management studies how some workplace practices, such as noncompete clauses, have a negative impact on employees. His research finds that when noncompetes are in place, employees will often stay at their current job—even if unhappy—simply to avoid any legal risk. If they leave, they often switch industries, to the detriment of their own economics and long-term potential as well as their industries.[13]) In short, policies that are designed to "keep" people ultimately hurt the employees' personal growth, the company's culture, and the industry these stars might defect from.

When I was at IBM, I had some good managers and advisers, and they encouraged me to take on special assignments and roles that provided visibility to senior corporate execs. I remember in my early career having built a very good reputation in computer security and being groomed to eventually move up the ranks into "corporate" in that field. The computer security department was moved into the IT department, and I acquired a new manager. Within a few months, he offered me a unique opportunity to move into financial systems in Boca Raton. I took the job excitedly, but I remember getting a very angry call from the head of security telling me that he was displeased that they were "losing" me.

The intrinsic problem with receiving coaching from your boss is that what might be a win for you is a loss for him or her. Companies don't want to relay how valuable you might be to someone else. And for someone who doesn't want to spend his or her entire career in one place, that makes mentoring as we know it a system that doesn't work very well.

Employees are aware that the system doesn't work. In a 2007 interactive poll by the Human Capital Institute about the business value of coaching or mentoring programs, participants were asked, "How effective is your organization in evaluating the business impact of coaching?" Sixty-six percent of respondents answered "not effective," 32 percent said "moderately effective," and 0 percent replied "very effective."[14] It's like the mainframe: it's outdated technology.

Mentoring 101 for Individuals

- Be open and welcoming to the concept of mentoring and coaching.
- Accept whatever help is available from your company.
- Solicit help from outside your company (ideally from trusted and knowledgeable sources).
- Develop a robust network that helps challenge and educate you about the possibilities that exist.
- Be willing to give advice and help to others.
- Understand that the way to access the best opportunities is to continue to execute on your current ones. Remember that you need to be voted on to the team every day.

MENTORING IN THE MODERN AGE

In the last decade, the social networking trend was born. Most if not all of us are familiar with Facebook, Twitter, and LinkedIn, but I'll admit I was initially turned off by these sites. As a busy executive, I spent much of my time focusing on big company issues and had little opportunity to network with random or long-lost acquaintances. The thought of putting my name out on LinkedIn so that folks could "network" with me on their terms was not appealing. I was amazed that people would put so much of their lives up on Facebook to share with mere acquaintances. I got most of my information from the web and newspapers.

Over time, though, I warmed up to the power of these networks as I realized that you can learn a lot quickly, and I developed protocols to protect my privacy. Soon, I realized I had more bandwidth than I'd thought and that I could handle the additional streams. Today, I get almost all of my latest-breaking information off of RSS feeds to my smartphone through Yahoo! and Twitter. I have more than one thousand contacts on LinkedIn. We are building special private networks within LinkedIn for my investment network (WIN) to collaborate on deals. I use Facebook. At my thirtieth high school reunion, no one knew how to find me; now, in time for my fortieth reunion, I am "friends" with more than fifty former classmates and can quickly get updated on their lives. I am able to keep up with many colleagues, and it adds a richness to know about their families and hobbies and to see them as people instead of just as work peers.

But enough about my personal life and productivity. Who would have envisioned the power of these networks to topple regimes around the world—Tunisia, Egypt, Libya, and who knows what other countries coming next? We're still in the early days of seeing the power of communities applied to companies, but it's evident that having these external networks vastly increases our work opportunities and options. This is the power of the new network.

Maintaining your own personal networks is much easier than ever before—even more so, it's becoming mandatory, as the people who do this well gain a significant advantage. Today, it's possible to access almost anyone—and that introduces incredible opportunities to build networks that can enable your careers. This external board of advisers can offer insight, direction, and introductions. These mentors can make a tremendous impact on your career and your life.

Much has been researched and written about the value of mentors at work. The relationship produces results: a large body of research demonstrates that when looking at career mentoring in terms of objective career success, better mentoring

Mentoring 101 for Companies

- If you don't have formal mentoring practices in place, implement them. Explore services like Menttium, which businesses use to provide mentors to employees.
- Expand your view of career development beyond your company's boundaries. For example, Bain & Company, a management consulting firm, has an excellent "externship" program in which consultants leave Bain to embark on a six-month working engagement at a company of their choice and then return to Bain. For employees, it's a low-risk way to gain experience in another company or role that interests them; for the company, it's a way to keep their best talent learning, challenged, tackling new experiences in new industries, and building specializations that they bring back to the company.
- Differentiate from other employers by truly putting the employee's career interests first.
- Understand that the best way to keep top employees is to ensure that they keep learning, growing, and being challenged. As an employer, you should operate as though your employees were deciding every day which company to join.

resulted in greater compensation, greater salary growth, and more promotions.[15] In addition, people benefit personally. Other studies have found that people were more clear about their "professional identity," meaning their unique talents and contributions at work as well as their personal values, strengths, and weaknesses.[16] Perhaps this is one of the reasons why the existence of a formal mentoring program is now a criterion against which the "Best Companies to Work For" are judged.[17]

So why do so few of us actually invest time in building relationships with mentors or coaches? When looking for advice, people most often go to the most convenient sources, but not the right ones. They haven't developed their own networks, so they ask for advice from whoever is right in front of them. Perhaps it's their boss, or colleagues at their company. Often it's their spouses, parents, or friends. Is this really the best way? Friends are great supporters, but do they really know how you can best leverage your skill set to advance in your changing industry—an industry that is different from theirs? Your mother might know you best and be your biggest fan, but does she really know how much you are worth in the marketplace?

And mentors at work? Besides the conflict of interest we already discussed, the way mentoring is approached inside companies is somewhat misguided. Too often, mentoring takes place at specified times, such as during a performance review. There are several problems with this. First of all, it happens infrequently, usually once or twice a year, which is not enough. Second, it's tied to compensation, which often makes the conversation very tense. That's not the right time to absorb advice. People do not feel receptive and open at a time when economics are at stake. Finally, this hierarchical boss-employee structure is more like a parent–child relationship, which is not what the mentoring relationship should replicate. It also can be ruled by politics rather than reality—that is, managers are instructed as to how to rank employees, and conversations are often dictated by the need for an employee to fit into a certain slot rather than by the truth about his or her performance.

It's best to discuss development and future goals in a different zone, when people are in a more receptive place and thinking about the future as opposed to being judged for the past.

Increasingly, next-generation companies are looking to new systems to change annual reviews and performance conversations to offer real-time feedback. Companies including Facebook, LivingSocial, and Spotify use social technologies such as Work.com to enable continuous advice, feedback, and recognition from people across all levels of the organization. This is a much more modern way to manage; it eliminates hierarchies and empowers and enables people to do their best work. Services like Work.com work within an organization, but as organizational walls break down further, we'll need to add external solutions to help identify mentors and connect with them.

Rebecca Graf, whose journey from Frame 1 to Frame 2 we followed in Chapter Five, and who had her share of moments in Frame 3 in the process, credits her very supportive friends who "got her through everything." Interestingly, these weren't Rebecca's former classmates or colleagues. In fact, some of them she never even met in person. As Rebecca began her career as a freelancer, she kept in touch with others in a similar position—a proofreader, an editor she met on an assignment, a classmate from her new online school—and built a network of people who had been through some comparable experiences and understood her goals. She kept in touch with them on Facebook and LinkedIn and via email and Skype, and says she would reach out to them when she was struggling with something—whether facing a plot snafu in her book or just needing some encouragement that it would work. "They are the reason I keep going," she says. These people also became trusted colleagues and cofounders in her new publishing endeavor.

As Rebecca has found, there's incredible merit to having a network of trusted advisers. In the process of writing this book, I looked for formal mentoring services that could help individuals build their own external networks to which they could go for insight, advice, and encouragement. There wasn't one service that was implemented broadly, so with a team of great entrepreneurs, I created a company, which connects people with experts who can give them appropriate advice. Think of it as eHarmony meets LinkedIn. Developing personal networks takes time and effort, but with social technologies it's easier than ever to find great mentors anywhere.

Too often we are guilty of making a terrible mistake: we keep our dreams and aspirations near and dear and are reluctant to share them with anyone. But when dreams are kept private, it's harder for them to take off. However, when we share them, amazing things can happen. Just ask Marc Benioff. When he started salesforce.com, he was, unlike many entrepreneurs, open to sharing his idea with trusted advisers and mentors and was thus able to tap into helpful expertise and a critical network. One of his mentors, a successful entrepreneur named Bobby Yazdani, the founder of Saba Software, introduced him to three talented developers who became Marc's cofounders and helped him build an incredible service and company. In fact, Marc has described meeting Parker Harris, one of the developers, as "the luckiest thing in my life." It wasn't luck; it was the result of Marc's articulating his vision and sharing it with a mentor who had experience, understanding, and a desire to help.

Marc Benioff's passion, energy, and enthusiasm for creating a whole new space called cloud computing inspire me. He had a vision for changing the software industry, and he didn't stop with cloud computing; he extended it to leverage social technologies. Most of all, he does everything with a big heart. In a similar vein, Steve Jobs's unbelievable dedication to creating great products that are focused on the customer experience has taught me many

---

REALITY CHECK
Don't Know People?

There are a lot of people who can inspire you, even if you don't know them. Coaching can come from all kinds of sources. It can come from reading about people or reading what they write. For example, I feel as though I know the late Stephen Covey, even though I've never met him. It can come from watching people you admire and respect. It's ideal when mentoring comes in the form of a direct relationship, but don't overlook people you may never meet. Be adventurous in thinking about finding answers from people whom you might not have to know to ask a question.

As much as I've learned from Meg Whitman and Marc Benioff, I've also learned from observing the careers of people I never met. I learned that CIOs came from the application side, not from the infrastructure side, and I adjusted my career path to mimic what I discovered to be the right path. A source like LinkedIn can help you understand career trajectories you may wish to emulate. For example, it will illustrate how many CEOs come from sales and marketing, not finance.

---

lessons. I admire Meg Whitman's ability to see what needs to be done, and to articulate it and inspire a team. She has a willingness to tackle hard and significant problems—which is why she ran for governor of California and why she is now heading up one of the world's biggest technology companies, Hewlett-Packard, even though she has already accomplished so much. These people have served as important mentors to me, and they have given me direction and purpose that has greatly affected my career and life.

The exercise in Appendix A on becoming the CEO of Your Own Destiny can help you determine and then articulate what you want to achieve at work and at home. Even though you might still be a long way from reaching your goals, sharing them with a trusted adviser is an important step to making them happen. Like my friend Marc Benioff, I believe that it's key.

Of course, the choice of the people with whom you share your goals is also an important consideration. Peter Gollwitzer, professor of psychology at New York University, who has called attention to some of the dangers of sharing goals too broadly, says that should you wish to make your goals public, you should tell only one or two people who "hold power over you" (metaphorically speaking), so that they will help you adhere to your intentions.[18] Jim Billington advised a network of three: "One mentor in your company, another in your field, and a third in your career together can form the narrow, but broadening, network that you need."[19] We know that the definition of "company" may be different now, but this guidance still holds. There's a big difference between telling a few carefully selected and cultivated mentors and a few hundred friends, colleagues, relatives, and Facebook connections.

Always aim high, but be very specific about what you want to achieve and how you will achieve it, and share these plans and aspirations with a few key advisers and mentors. Doing so makes you more committed and gets others invested in seeing you reach your dreams.

THERE'S NOTHING TO FEAR (BUT FEAR)

I get inspired by doing new and innovative things, but I know that not everyone is as enthusiastic as I am about this. The tougher the challenges, the more intractable the resistance to change can be. And when it comes to revolutionizing work both on a micro and a macro level, there are many intimidating roadblocks.

Our technology and our digital lives have been advancing at a breakneck pace, and we have seen some of the intricate challenges that our social, business, and policy leaders are facing to keep up with this changing world. Our human hardwiring makes us fear behavioral change, and the way our businesses are structured makes it hard for management both to grant new freedoms to workers and to institute dramatic changes as a company. As technology and policy move forward, our first reactions are often based on fear. We become more protective of the old ways of doing things and often resist innovation and change.

Although we are seeing an increase in telecommuting and flex hours, corporations for the most part still adhere to yesterday's management principles, which are poorly suited for today's world. When it comes to adopting the less traditional and more innovative programs that will enable us to fix work, the most commonly cited obstacle is lack of management buy-in. Managers fear that employees, left unmonitored, will not work as hard as they otherwise would. That's baloney, though. Study after study demonstrates that people who work from home are more productive than their office counterparts. Why? In part it is because home-based workers have fewer interruptions, as they aren't distracted by chitchat, coffee breaks, birthday parties, fantasy football pools, and all the black holes that suck time out of every day in the office. Amazingly, office employees admit to wasting two hours a day outside of lunch and scheduled breaks. It adds up: businesses lose $600 billion a year in workplace distractions.[20]

We have to address the serious problems with the world of work and stop living in fear of failure and fear of change. We have to take a How Can I? approach. Jeremy Lin, formerly of the New

York Knicks and now with the Houston Rockets, moved from an obscure backup to a team star, and even though his coaches couldn't believe how far he'd come, it wasn't all that "Lin-sane." Lin wasn't living in Frame 3, filled with bitterness and a crabby attitude when he was sitting on the bench. He was always working on bettering himself to get where he wanted to be. He started practice early every morning—hours before his former teammates rolled in. With hard work, dedication, and a new can-do attitude, we can change our lives and take charge of our destinies.

One of the most important lessons I've learned in my career is that "miracles" happen every day in the workplace. I've been lucky enough to experience several in my career. When I went to eBay in 1999, the company was battling some significant technology issues. Many people said I was crazy to join in the midst of such turmoil. Certainly during those dark days at eBay, no one believed the company would evolve into the world's largest online marketplace and transform the world of e-commerce. But the real miracle I witnessed was not eBay's rise to greatness but rather the many moments when I saw teams unleash their potential and brilliantly solve what was previously deemed impossible.

At the time, the site's architecture couldn't handle the company's sudden growth, and the site kept crashing. At its worst, there was a twenty-two-hour outage that nearly destroyed the company. Things were so bad that employees put paper over the windows to keep the reporters from seeing in. Users grew wary, and the stock tanked.

There was a traditional way that these issues were handled: stop everything and figure out exactly what was bringing down the system. No changes. No new code. No innovation until the system was stabilized. But in an online world, that old model didn't make sense. Why did a company have to choose between stabilization and innovation when it really needed both? I realized that we needed reliability and new features that could handle increased volume. We had previously seen the dangers of making the wrong choices when eBay froze product development for three months to stabilize and we fell far behind in our development plan. In those few months, Yahoo! went into Japan and built the market, which they still dominate today.

This time we turned our back on the old-fashioned way and embraced the Spirit of "And": we committed to stabilizing the system AND making it better. (We also refunded sellers who had live auctions at the time the site went down.) As we restored trust with users and our partners, we also earned a better relationship with Wall Street.

I again saw a tech team achieve greatness against the odds when we had issues with getting search to scale at the massive rates at which we were bringing in new products. It would take twenty-four hours to index description listings before they went live, angering sellers who were paying for the service. In addition, the infrastructure updates cost the company millions. Solving this technology puzzle was not eBay's core competency, so the management team looked to buy a solution rather than build it. We approached Google and Yahoo!, but ultimately, given the uniqueness of our needs and the urgency of the situation, we decided to build it ourselves. The developer team knew its mission and didn't have to be driven hard. They were self-motivated and inspired and engaged to create change. That self-direction—as opposed to command-and-control pressure from above—made all the difference. What should have been a twelve- to eighteen-month project was achieved in two months. The newly built solution allowed us to get listings up in minutes and saved us millions of dollars.

My most favorite miracle at eBay, though, was what the team accomplished in response to 9/11. Moments after the attack, I got a call from eBay's trust and safety division: someone had tried to auction rubble from the Twin Towers on our site. It was our policy not to allow sellers to profit from disasters, but we realized that something bigger could be done than just stopping the vulture postings. That afternoon, Governor Pataki called and asked if we could auction items that were given to the state of New York and then send the proceeds to charities. What about doing something more compelling, we asked? What about firing up our community of sellers to help set up an auction and raise money for victims of the disaster?

We had never done a project like this, which we soon named Auction for America. We needed to get toll-free 800 numbers and create the capability for people to answer the calls. (Previously we had relied on emails.) There were also tax considerations and government regulatory issues and approvals we needed. And on top of that, the coding itself was massively complex. In the past, this would have taken us six months, but we didn't have that kind of time. And as it turned out—as the team showed us—we didn't need it.

We worked night and day, literally, for four nights, and maybe that sounds hellacious, but it wasn't. In that time we built a fully functioning auction site. Jay Leno donated his motorcycles, and Bo Derek donated her bathing suits. By letting go of the old way of doing things and unleashing the potential of the team and the community, we raised $25 million.

Every day I am inspired by what's possible. People thought it was impossible to walk on the moon, get fingers to grow back, or talk to anyone in the world in real time through the computer. I've been fortunate enough to learn from some of the best "and" entrepreneurs. And the results are impressive: Omar Hamoui dropped out of Wharton to start AdMob AND transformed an industry in eighteen months (and had two industry titans fight over his company in their quest to dominate the mobile landscape). Marc Benioff quit an executive post at Oracle to change the enterprise software industry AND pioneered a phenomenon now known as cloud computing.

There's a false notion that success is a zero-sum game. That to win in our careers we have to give up family. That to work hard we have to sacrifice sleep. That to be successful we must take (or borrow or steal) from somewhere else in our lives. It's just not the case. Working harder is not a sustainable solution, and it's not how people meet their destiny. It's time to get more creative. Instead of choosing one thing we love over something else we love, we must ask, "How can I do both?" And, then, we can find solutions (perhaps by eliminating something we hate, like commuting).

There's never been a better time to change the way you think. Replace every "I can't" with "How can I?" This might sound like semantics, but I promise that this shift in thinking will bring whatever you want to accomplish much closer to reality. Things that you thought would take six months might take six weeks, or even six days.

Where do you see yourself in nine months, two years, and five years? Where do you see yourself in the future? I think that in the future, companies will compete better, individuals will have great careers, and the planet will be sustainable. I urge you to join me. It's much more rewarding to be inspired by all that you can do rather than to be afraid that you can't.

ADVICE FOR POWERING OUT OF FRAME 3

Focus on being voted on to the team every day. Make sure you do something every day to show others you deserve to be part of their team. (This same rule applies to companies if they want to keep great talent.)

It's all about integrity. Do what you say. Say what you do. Always act in a way that makes people remember you positively. For my life, my test involves an imagined simple interaction with a former colleague or employee twenty-five years from now. I am sitting on a park bench. I'm no longer the boss. I no longer can give the person a job or a promotion, so there is really no reward for being nice to me. Will this person come up to me sitting on that bench, happy to see me again, or will he or she pretend not to notice me and walk by?

Have a great attitude. You might be brilliant, but if you are hard to manage, it's easy to find someone else. You have to be fun and easy to work with.

Work for a higher purpose. At eBay, we didn't sell stuff from people's attics. We created e-commerce and empowered a generation of entrepreneurs. No matter what your job is, understand that its impact is broader than making money. You will find more meaning in what you do every day, and a higher purpose will guide you through the inevitable tough days.

Pick your battles. There are a million things to be upset about in any work situation. Fight only about things that are really important and that will move the needle.

Don't be afraid of change. As you advance, don't look back and wish for things to be the way they used to be. When I joined eBay, the company was at a few hundred million in revenue. This is kind of hilarious to think about now, but people who had been there since the beginning would say, "This was so much more fun when we were smaller." Well, companies don't stay the same size: they grow or they shrink. I'd rather grow.

Be brutally honest with yourself. Be harder on yourself than anyone else will be on you. Know your strengths and weaknesses.

Don't confuse action for traction. Focus on outcomes, not face time. So many people work very hard and are utterly exhausted, yet they don't achieve anything that will matter in the long run. So how do you know where to focus your energies?

Focus on expanding your sphere of influence. Don't get upset about things over which you have no control. If you invest your energy into expanding your sphere of influence, you can make a dramatic impact over more zones.

Take time to sit back and reflect on where you are and where you want to be. Make time for a "compass check." It is so easy to fall into a routine and not take the time to see if you are heading where you want to go. Assessing your career goals shouldn't just be tied to birthday milestones; use the exercise in Appendix A to help you outline your goals and aspirations.

Be brave and be bold. Most things worth doing are hard. Successful people get to where they are in their careers because they make the hard appear easy.

7

Frame 4: The Aspiring Entrepreneur

I grew up in the generation that experienced Woodstock, the era that celebrated personal freedom—yet, ironically, my peers jumped into companies and corporate ladders and defined hierarchies, and thought it was fantastic. It was cool to work at IBM, and we were blessed to get a job there.

It's so different now. Today's generation of people between the ages of twenty-five and thirty-five are starting businesses at three times the rate that Baby Boomers did at the same age.[1] And many people today—especially Gen X and Gen Y and younger—cringe at the thought of working for a big company. Seventy percent of Xers prefer to work independently. Of those who like being their own boss, 81 percent say the reason is that they value having control over their work, according to Center for Talent Innovation data.[2]

For today's youngest people entering the workforce, this notion is even more amplified. Gen Y aspires more to entrepreneurship than to rising in established corporate ranks. In Silicon Valley, the nexus of start-ups, recent graduates of Stanford University considered taking a corporate job, even from the hottest companies like Facebook, Twitter, or Google, a "backup plan."[3] Plan A was to start their own companies. Now, more than ever, Stanford MBAs are rejecting corporate jobs and instead launching their own enterprises. An all-time high of 16 percent of the class of 2011 chose to start their own companies at graduation. This reflects a threefold increase from only 5 percent in the early 1990s and is a third higher than the 12 percent peak during the dot-com bubble.[4] We are also seeing a generational shift among MBAs, who are preferring to work for smaller companies or start-ups—places defined by a more entrepreneurial culture, with structures they describe as "flat" and "nonhierarchical" and that promote personal responsibility, ownership, flexibility, and mentorship.[5]

I'm in awe of all of this—I admire this entrepreneurial mind-set and believe in entrepreneurship as the answer to solving many of the world's issues. But unfortunately the reality is that sometimes dreams and drive aren't enough for success.

I've seen a number of people with great ideas and great ambition and who work extremely hard, but who don't see their careers or businesses take off. There are infinite reasons: too much competition; the product or value proposition isn't right; the market isn't ready. This is Frame 4. People in Frame 4 have the right attitude, but they are not achieving the economics they need to make everything work.

Life in Frame 2, living as the CEO of Your Own Destiny, carries unprecedented responsibility. When you are in the center of Frame 2 as an entrepreneur or independent contractor, you are responsible for paying for your own health care; there are no paid sick days or vacation days; and in some states, such as New York, there's an additional tax for being self-employed. All of this can be challenging and costly. These factors are what makes Frame 4 such a common pit stop for so many people on their way to Frame 2.

The Framework: Where Do You See Yourself?

	Paternalistic Era	The Age of Entrepreneurship
Meritocracy: feels personally invested, proactive, positive, willing	**Frame 1** **Company Man or Woman** • You are a high achiever. • You have a great attitude. • You are on a promotion track. • You have only as much future as the company you are with. **Recommendation:** *Continue your emphasis on high performance, but broaden your view of your career beyond the constraints of any one company.*	**Frame 2** **CEO of Your Own Destiny** • You are highly successful. • You are self-aware. • You love the freedom this choice has given you. • You opt in to being fully on the team every day. • You work to build a network outside the office "walls." • You have great and fulfilling career options. **Recommendation:** *You can work for yourself or a corporation and still be the CEO of Your Own Destiny. This is the sweet spot for the future of work.*
Entitlement: feels deserving, frustrated, critical	**Frame 3** **Disenchanted Employee** • You are waiting to be discovered or recognized. • You can't understand why others don't understand how good you are. • You are not progressing in your career at the speed you expected. • You believe your circumstances to be someone else's problem. **Recommendation:** *Take a meaningful look at what you want to achieve and the steps you will take to achieve it.*	**Frame 4** **Aspiring Entrepreneur** • You fully embrace controlling your own destiny. • You don't have enough work to do on the terms you are willing to do it. • You may not be addressing the gaps between your desires and your skills. **Recommendation:** *Reassess your value proposition to understand why your view of your value is not aligned with your current environment; make appropriate course corrections.*

It's my hope that people in Frame 4 are in this box only temporarily, but the danger is that they stagnate here and then don't acquire some of the skills and experience that will be necessary to achieve economic success. Oftentimes, the path out of Frame 4 is not a nonstop trip to Frame 2, but involves making compromises, such as taking another job to make ends meet, going back to school to gain new skills, or going to a corporate job to gain necessary experience.

I was in Frame 4 at a crucial point in my career when I jumped from blue-collar work as a security guard to a white-collar job in product and computer security. It was a great opportunity in the long term, but it came with a significant economic cost in the short term. The new job was much better, but ironically, the pay at the old job was better. As a security guard, I worked the second shift, 4 PM to midnight, which carried a 10 percent premium in pay because of the inconvenience of working nights. The job required seven-day coverage (weekends off were sporadic); working on Saturdays earned me time-and-a-half, and working Sundays earned me double time. Holidays paid double time-and-a-half. None of this included overtime, and I was an overtime machine, willing to work whenever there was a need. All in all, I made almost twice my base pay because of the extra incentives.

Although the new white-collar job came with a better base salary, I lost thousands of dollars in income I had made in overtime. I was accustomed to that money, and I had to take a second job at JC Penney to make up for the lost income and maintain the lifestyle we were living. I worked at IBM in the day, and after hours worked in the shipping area, rang up purchases, and assembled gas grills and patio furniture in the JC Penney outdoor department during nights and on the weekends. It was humbling when people I knew from IBM came in and asked, "What are you doing here?"

I don't regret making that decision and sacrificing income for opportunity. It was the right decision for my family and for me. At the same time, I took classes to learn programming and to make me more marketable. I knew my future was bright, although in the present I was working harder and was worse off economically. I did not stay in this Frame 4 state for too long: I received several promotions, and within a year or two the economics started to work, and I no longer had to supplement my income with another job.

So You Think You Can Be an Entrepreneur?

Technology has changed how we communicate and work— largely eradicating the need for working in one place or for set hours. The Internet and the advent of cloud computing have made software dramatically less expensive than it was even a few years ago. For example, just a decade ago, the cost to run a basic Internet application was approximately $150,000 a month. Running that same application today in Amazon's cloud costs hundreds or a few thousand dollars at the most. With that change, people can start their own companies faster and more cheaply and easily than ever before. It's also easier for people to work for themselves as independent contractors.

And today, more than ever, people want to be their own boss. According to a survey sponsored by Kelly Services, 18 percent of the Gen X workforce described its status as "free agent." Only three years later, in 2011, that number rose to 38 percent—a more than 100 percent increase.[6]

The climate has never been better for entrepreneurs, but the startling reality is that for the past thirty years, the failure rate of new businesses hasn't changed—and it's pretty depressing. Whatever way you look at it, the fact is, most companies fail. Data from the Small Business Administration and the Bureau

REALITY CHECK

Although many young people in Silicon Valley don't want corporate jobs, the reality is that many corporate jobs aren't hiring as much in this economy, and there are hoards of recent graduates who would love these jobs. My advice is to get busy and get to work. If you can't find a job that you are qualified for, find a company you admire and take a lesser job to gain experience and get your foot in the door. If that doesn't work, start freelancing on one of the many sites that are out there, such as Elance, LiveOps, or oDesk, where you can connect to great work, learn about what's hot, and continue to hone your skills.

of Labor Statistics consistently show that approximately half of new start-ups no longer exist after five years, and that approximately two-thirds will cease to be in operation ten years after founding.[7] Dane Stangler of the Kauffman Foundation notes that approximately five hundred thousand new firms are created every year and that after five years, fewer than half of these companies will remain.[8] Shikhar Ghosh, a senior lecturer at the Harvard Business School, looks at start-ups that take in outside money and finds that 30 to 40 percent fail. He defines failure as liquidating all assets, with investors losing most or all the money they put into the company. If failure is defined as not realizing the projected return on investment, then the failure rate is 70 to 80 percent.[9]

And the start-ups that get big—really big, Amazon or eBay or Google or salesforce.com big, represent only a small sliver of total businesses. Of all of the technology companies started in the United States in any one year, only approximately fifteen ever generate $100 million in annual revenue. Those fifteen companies will ultimately be responsible for 97 percent of the market capitalization of the entire set of companies started that year.[10] The truth is, not everyone is born to be an entrepreneur. It's incredibly hard work. Marc Andreessen, the famed entrepreneur turned legendary venture capitalist, famously told then-CEO of Loudcloud (and now business partner) Ben Horowitz that when it comes to starting a company, "You only ever experience two emotions: euphoria and terror. And I find that lack of sleep enhances them both."[11] Eddy Lu, the entrepreneur who slept in his car when he started Grubwithus and was ferociously trying to make ends meet, couldn't agree more. "It's not for everyone," he says.

What about if you want to be the CEO of Your Own Destiny, but not necessarily the CEO of your own company? The statistics here are similarly discouraging. The number of independent contractors is growing, but that doesn't ensure individual success. Being a free agent can be especially challenging, especially in the beginning. Some 90 percent of the people who start down the path of affiliating with and providing work through companies like LiveOps and SupportSpace do not make it to the point of earning even a few hundred dollars a month for several months, according to Tim Whipple, who managed our community of twenty thousand independent agents at LiveOps for seven years and who now manages a community of two thousand independent tech support experts at SupportSpace. Of the approximately 10 percent who do make it to that point, fewer than 20 percent earn money equivalent to full-time employment. It's important to note that this isn't because the work isn't necessarily there but because freelancers and independent contractors often are actually choosing to work a part-time schedule. Nevertheless, the takeaway is that in most cases, the economic gain, at least initially, will likely be less than before.

Sara Horowitz, who runs Freelancers Union, doesn't have exact figures on freelancer failure rates, but believes that the main reason contractors fail is that current laws and practices expect contractors to be experts in all aspects of the business process. Whereas an employee can focus or specialize on a particular topic (for example, marketing), contractors are forced to master these topics as well as benefits, HR, legal, production, and so on. This, coupled with the episodic, feast-or-famine nature of contract work, contributes to the challenges of succeeding as a freelancer.

The good news is that for those who do make it, living as the CEO of Your Own Destiny becomes the only way. We have less than 10 percent attrition at LiveOps after agents make it past their first thirty days, or three hundred calls. oDesk, the world's largest and fastest-growing online workplace, which has more than two million contractors who have created profiles, about four hundred thousand job posts, and about seventy thousand active billing contractors a quarter, reports that contractors who stick with it actually find working this way to be more financially lucrative. After one year on oDesk, people's average wage increases by 60 percent; after three years, it increases 190 percent, according to oDesk CEO Gary Swart. Contractors on oDesk work both part-time and full-time, some choosing to work as much as eighty hours a week.

There is often a challenging in-between period, a ramp-up to success, which is very much the definition of Frame 4, but after a certain investment in time (thirty days to one year) and in gaining experience, independent contractors are able to move into—and remain—in Frame 2. And this is a global phenomenon. Marcel Morgan, a Jamaican computer programmer, was not getting the

Typical Pitfalls for a Freelancer or Independent Contractor

- Has difficulty dealing with the lack of structure and account-ability
- Is too easily distracted in a nonstructured environment
- Makes insufficient financial investment in business tools needed to optimize the work
- Is not willing to invest time in the learning or certification needed to do well
- Enters contracts with work providers who overpromise or are misleading about the terms of work or type of work, or does so without really understanding the nature of the work or the outcomes needed to succeed
- Does not sufficiently network with independent contractors who are already succeeding at the same type of work to learn best practices and secrets of success
- Is unable to master the myriad necessary business skills that have nothing to do with the freelancer's core competency
- Neglects to find mentors and build a support network that will help the contractor stay on course and continuously improve

Source: Tim Whipple, VP Service Operations at SupportSpace and former VP Service Delivery for LiveOps.

types of programming and Web development projects that he wanted in his corporate job, so he started looking for part-time work on oDesk in 2010. He worked hard to build his client list and soon left his job to work full-time as an independent contractor. "It was a real shock to my friends to quit the highest-paying job in Jamaica, but I wanted to start my own business and work on my own terms," he says. It has paid off. He estimates his income to be at least 20 percent higher than his full-time corporate job,

Do You Want to Be Your Own Boss?

You get the technology, but what about the work practices? Answer these questions to see if you are ready to reframe the way you work.

1. Do you have marketable relevant skills?
2. Are you self-directed and highly productive when you are on your own?
3. Do you crave freedom?
4. Do you have the ability to market yourself?
5. Do you embrace continuous learning and improvement?
6. Are you active in social media, such as LinkedIn, Facebook, and Twitter?
7. Are you willing to deal with administration (billing, collections, payroll)?
8. Are you technically savvy enough to leverage the new tools available?
9. Are you willing to live without entitlements and benefits (like paid vacations and company-paid health care)?

Did you answer yes to most of these questions? If so, you have the Frame 2 mind-set and are ready for the freedom and opportunity that being the CEO of Your Own Destiny will provide. Go back and look at your "no" responses (if there were any) and determine what you need to do to move them to yes. This will help move you from Frame 4 to Frame 2.

assuming that he works enough hours for the year; so far, he is on target to achieve that.

Many of the founders of today's hottest businesses spent some time in Frame 4 before getting to the promised land of Frame 2. Ben Silbermann, the founder and CEO of Pinterest, always idolized entrepreneurs (he says he thought they were cool the way people think basketball players are cool), but instead of striking out on his own, he took a job at an IT consulting firm when he graduated college and then went to Google, where he worked for the display advertising group. (Frame 1 all the way, he thought "Google was the coolest place."[12]) He imbibed everything he could from the company—learning to think big and embracing the importance of working with very smart people. "Google had the audacity to think at a really big scale . . . It was inspiring," he said.[13]

But he wanted to build something on his own, though he wasn't sure what. He resigned and lived off his personal savings while making iPhone apps with a college friend. They weren't successful, and he was living in Frame 4—having a big vision, but not a big paycheck. "I've worked on products where they go down in the middle of the night and no one notices," he says of this time.

None of those apps went very far, and neither did Pinterest in the beginning. The company, which launched in an apartment in March 2010, had a low user base and very little engagement. After nine months, the site had less than ten thousand users, and many weren't using it very frequently. "It was like stealth without us trying to be stealth," he said. But he found the idea of telling people he failed to be too embarrassing, so he continued to tinker and improve the site. He obsessed over making it right, and after some media attention in June 2011, the site began to reach a tipping point. Today, Pinterest has more than twenty million users[14] and is one of the fastest-growing social services in the world. Ben Silbermann's investment in making the site better and his How Can I? attitude transitioned him out of Frame 4 and into Frame 2.

Maybe you have an idea, but it hasn't achieved the traction you anticipated. You are living in Frame 4. How do you know whether to keep going or to make a change? You might modify the product, change how you market or distribute it, or examine how external events (technology or regulatory changes, for example) affect it.

Ben Silbermann made incremental changes to improve Pinterest, but he kept the vision and didn't pivot from the idea of a social bulletin board. Marc Benioff evolved salesforce.com by bringing popular consumer trends to the enterprise, but never pivoted away from his idea of making software easier, more accessible, and more democratic for businesses.

Other entrepreneurs have executed a "big pivot," changing everything about the product. Instagram, which started as Burbn, a mobile social check-in app with game features, saw that the photo sharing feature was where the majority of its user engagement came from, and pivoted before launch; Fab, the popular design-focused e-commerce site, was a daily deal site before it became a design-focused storefront.[15] Switch Video started as Switch Fuel with a vision to make energy out of switchgrass, but its explanatory video opened up new opportunities, and producing videos became the new business. Badgeville was originally called Credd and was a consumer website focused on online reputation. "People weren't really excited at all and thought it was a dumb idea. I had to go back to the drawing board," says Kris Duggan, CEO. Kris thought about his strengths, which were more in the enterprise space than the consumer space, and transformed the company to play into his "superpowers." He also talked to leaders at more than one hundred companies to investigate what kind of service they needed. He used that insight and research to create a product that people wanted.

Keep on Trucking, Pivot, or Shut It Down?

There are several things to check before knowing whether to pivot:

- How long do you have to live? How much cash do you have to continue pursuing your dream? Can you raise more money based on the traction you have?
- Is there traction at all? Are you building something that people like? How certain are you that this will be a winnable market? Are you early? Late? Is your timing off?
- Can you do something that has much more relevance? Have you developed any new insights which demonstrate that you should be chasing something else?
- How do you want to treat shareholders who have invested in you, when you are unsure of where you want to go? Are you able to provide a return to shareholders rather than just burn through the cash?

Amazon founder and CEO Jeff Bezos calls this investigate-everything process the "regret-minimization framework," urging you to explore all the plausible possibilities—spending extra time figuring out if the idea is worth it, rather than later regretting that you gave up too early or didn't delve deep enough.[16]

THE EXPERIENCE ISSUE

Academic research suggests a basic reason why so many start-ups fail: a large number of inexperienced entrepreneurs start businesses that shouldn't be founded in industries that are unfavorable to new companies.[17]

I worry about people who just want to be entrepreneurs but haven't taken the time to hone their skills so that they are ready for Frame 2. Frame 2 is the destination, but the fact is, no one starts in Frame 2—it is the result of hard work, experience, and determination. Arriving in Frame 2 is not solely about luck, and it often does have a lot to do with patience.

Perhaps no one demonstrates this better than Kris Duggan, the CEO of Badgeville. (Disclosure: I was an early investor in Badgeville.) Kris, who was born in Australia and moved here when he was five, always wanted to be an entrepreneur. His father moved the family to the United States for his corporate job and to pursue the American Dream—and he did, starting a company when he was in his forties, which he sold to a public company.

Kris looked to his dad as a role model in entrepreneurship. After he earned his MBA, he started his own company, the Oz Network, which was like Yahoo! for Australia. He sold the company for $5 million when he was twenty-six years old.

From there he took a path that is unusual—but that was highly instrumental in paving the way for future success. Instead of rushing to start another company, he intelligently built his resume—and experience. Kris says that one of his mentors, his brother-in-law, a venture capitalist who meets with countless entrepreneurs, guided him on this path. "Are you going to invest in yourself or cash out on yourself?" he asked. Kris knew he wasn't yet ready to swing for the fences with a new idea. He had more to learn.

He worked for several early start-ups, where he gained knowledge about how small companies got funded and operated. After a few years and a few start-ups, he had gained entrepreneurial experience, but lacked large-company experience (something he needed, considering that if starts-ups are successful they one day become large companies). He went to WebEx, which had several hundred people at the time. Although Kris went to a bigger company and was very successful there—he started as a sales rep and received several promotions, eventually rising to a top-performing director—he wasn't living in Frame 1 as a Company Man. He was a dedicated and diligent employee, but he possessed a Frame 2 mind-set, as he was there not to ensure security but to gain skills. He says that on the first day, he was already thinking about leaving, deciding he wouldn't stay more than three years. In fact, Kris did leave in his third year, having achieved everything he came to WebEx to accomplish. He had learned about sales, management, leading a team, establishing a culture, setting a vision, and adhering to corporate values—skills that would be necessary later in his career. "I would not have known any of these things had I went straight to start my own company," Kris says. "The WebEx experience is applicable every day."

Kris says that he knew he was an entrepreneur at heart, but he still wasn't ready to start something. He wanted to be closer to the idea process than a big company allowed, so he went to a small software company, where he grew the sales team and revenue and learned what worked and what didn't. After three years there, he felt he was ready—he'd gained hands-on operating management skills, discipline, and training—and he left, with no idea for a company, but with the confidence, gained from experience, that he could build something successful.

"Raw talent will get you far, but it can't take you all the way," says Kris. "You need to have an entrepreneurial spirit, but you also need experience." Looking back, Kris says he "invested" in himself. "Being patient has been helpful in doing it right."

He certainly has done it right. Badgeville, which makes software to inspire people to be more productive, was launched in September 2010 with one employee (Kris). It now employs seventy people and has 150 customers, including Barnes & Noble, Dell, and IBM, which use the service to motivate and engage employees; the company does $10–$15 million in sales. Kris is not only succeeding as the CEO of his own destiny but also helping companies manage employees in a way that is more modern and effective.

THE PATH OUT OF FRAME 4: PLAN AHEAD

Leaving the trappings of a corporate job can be difficult economically. The key to easing the transition and increasing the chance of ultimate success lies in planning ahead:

- Retool your skill set: take classes or look for jobs that will develop and increase your skills.
- Save money. Create a plan to save. Think about bonuses, and earmark any extra earnings to help things stay afloat during this time of transition. Exit your job with a reasonable amount of savings; financial planners usually recommend six months of expenses.
- Reduce expenses; live on less.
- Determine your health care needs and your health care plan, as this will not be supplemented by an employer. Thankfully, this will become far less of an issue with Obamacare, as everyone will have access to insurance, although if you're self-employed, you will still have to pay for yourself (unless you are on welfare). Also consider looking to industry organizations. Freelancers Union provides independent workers with high-quality, affordable,

and portable health insurance. In 2012, it was selected to sponsor nonprofit, consumer-driven health plans in New York, New Jersey, and Oregon, with $340 million in federal funding. Launching in 2014, the plans will expand health care to the nation's forty-two million independent workers.

- Focus on retirement planning. Working for yourself means there's no company pension plan or matching 401(k). SEP-IRAs are a good tax-deferred way for self-employed people to save for retirement.

- Understand that sole proprietorship doesn't come with paid holidays, vacation days, or sick days. Plan ahead and budget for these things.

8

The Age of Entrepreneurship

The Millennials already account for forty million in the workforce, and they are set to become America's first hundred-million-member generation. How they grew up—with mobile devices, online access, and social media—influences the way they work.[1] And it's influencing the way everyone will work.

Although I advocate the benefits of working as an independent contractor, I understand that doing so is a stretch for many people. I think there is a much larger number of workers who operate with a Frame 2 mentality but have chosen to work for companies for various reasons. There's the nasty reality that many new companies fail, which introduces the possibility of not being able to provide for your family or build an appropriate livelihood. Some people might want the perks of corporate life such as paid vacations and health care and retirement planning. For these reasons, I believe that many people will still work for companies, but I also believe that how they do that must change.

Today's workforce is looking for a new way to engage with work, and traditional employers must recognize that. Similarly, start-ups—which if successful, will also become big companies—must also establish a modern culture that appeals to today's talent. Today's companies need to appeal to today's modern workforce—not treat people the same way I was treated when I started working.

The problem is that many employers still don't understand and don't value the mind-set of this new generation and how it is revolutionizing the way we work. Many companies, such as Facebook, salesforce.com, Google, and LinkedIn, as well as countless start-ups, understand that there is a huge war for talent under way, and they want their key people to feel challenged and proud of their employer. They offer incredible perks, like massage services and pet-friendly policies, and give them time to work on their own ideas. These companies have also figured out how to connect to them, embracing such practices as more flexible hours, valuing outcomes over attendance, and employing the latest technology. All companies will have to undergo a similar shift, or they will miss out on working with the talent that will dominate the workforce.

Some employers are still turned off by the Millennial's high opinion of itself and its impatience to get to where it wants to be, but in fact this generation has significant contributions to offer, and its philosophy that every individual is in charge of his or her own fate is a new worldview that corporations will need to embrace. I am amazed when some companies don't let their employees access Facebook or Twitter from their work environments. People work from home and after hours, and they can catch up anytime through Facebook and their smartphones. Limiting network access to these services inside a company is just lame. We should be holding people accountable for outcomes and results, not dictating what they can do when. It is this kind of behavior that chases young people away from companies.

One aspect of work that employers have to reevaluate and, in many cases, change, is the way they recognize employees.

More than anything, today's employees want to see the difference they make in their organization and be recognized for it. In fact, a study conducted by the Gallup Organization of more than eighty thousand employees found that 82 percent of employees surveyed said that recognition motivates them to improve their job performance. It found that one of the top twelve key factors in securing employee engagement is regular praise and recognition from managers. Traditional service awards like gold watches and tie tacks don't motivate or engage employees because there is no meaningful recognition behind the one-time reward, the study concluded.[2]

We are seeing new ways to recognize employees proliferate in the workplace. Take, for example, Work.com, a service that uses social technologies to transform the way companies recognize and reward their employees. (Disclosure: I invested in this service, formerly called Rypple, and in 2012 it was acquired by salesforce.com.) Work.com allows for bits of real-time feedback, goal setting, coaching praise, and public recognition for team members. People feel more engaged and passionate about their work when they feel more valued. Making it easier to recognize good work and deliver praise goes a long way to inspiring employee and company success. With Work.com, instead of waiting for the dreaded annual or semiannual performance review, managers can give continuous feedback, coaching, and praise at anytime, not just at an artificially appointed review period. There are a variety of ways this can be delivered, in the form of an electronic note, or even a badge that will go on a worker's profile. (This evokes social gaming practices, and the so-called gamification of the enterprise is one trend we'll continue to see take off.) Real-time and public recognition makes sense—it happens when the feedback is still relevant and when changes can be more easily implemented. That creates a much more iterative and agile culture. Using a technology that is social, and open for everyone to see, brings teams together and helps them stay focused on what matters. Companies like Gilt, Facebook, Mozilla, and Zendesk all use Work.com to approach performance management in a different way, one that actually helps improve performance of their employees—and ultimately the entire company. This is just one of the many new tools available to businesses, to satisfy the next generation of workers who care more about being publicly acknowledged for their contributions with instant recognition than waiting a year for a performance review.

Similarly, Kris Duggan's company, Badgeville, is also finding success changing how companies approach performance management. With the traditional way of working, "You don't know how you're doing relative to goals or relative to others. There's no feedback loop in place to drive performance. Maybe you get an annual review, but with work more distributed and more people telecommuting, there's a gap in people knowing how they are doing," says Kris. A service like Badgeville uses principles of gamification to connect, engage, encourage, and motivate people to perform and provides transparency into how everyone is doing. It enables a system of meritocracy, which, as I discussed previously in this book, will define the workplace of the future. It's already resonating—the company's valuation is one hundred times that of when it started.

THE NEW NEW COMPANY

Companies that we had never heard of a few years ago—Facebook, Foursquare, and Twitter—quickly became the hot places to work because in addition to creating innovative products and services, they understood the needs of today's workers and created cultures that attracted and retained them. Putting it simply, these cultures are more entrepreneurial. Hierarchies are less important.

Although operating as a corporation, Facebook has done an excellent job of creating a culture that epitomizes the Age of Entrepreneurship. It does not assign opportunity based on seniority or title or ability to play office politics, but affords everyone the same chance to make a meaningful contribution.

One practice that perhaps highlights this best is Bootcamp, where every new engineer, whether a former VP from VMware or a recent college graduate, experiences the same six-week onboarding program. From day one, it gets engineers immersed in the code, offers insight into finding the highest-impact projects, and encourages the embracing of the Facebook philosophy (what they call "Move fast and break things"). The system is a meritocracy. The company expects engineers get their hands dirty with real assignments from the first time they boot up, and everyone is tasked with making a change to the live site within his or her first week. What is perhaps most unusual—and really demonstrates how even as employees, Facebookers are in charge of their own destiny—is that at the end of Bootcamp, engineers aren't assigned a team; they choose one. This approach works for the employee, and it works for Facebook. VP of engineering Mike Schroepfer explains, "We know they'll be happier when they work on something that they have passion for, and no doubt that 'passion multiplier' will yield far better products."

To this end, the company does something else unique. Instead of keeping people on a project when they're doing a good job—where conventional wisdom would want them to stay at all costs—Facebook tells them to leave. Engineers who have been on the same project for twelve to eighteen months are encouraged to take a "hackamonth"—to leave their current project and work on something in a completely different area. (This is a good way to prevent anyone from falling into Frame 3.) Engineers can opt out, but most don't. Offering people an opportunity to switch technical disciplines and collaborate with different teams is important. Facebook has also found that a month is a significant amount of time to get something meaningful done: an update to the Facebook iPhone app was achieved during a hackamonth, as were crucial improvements in overall site performance.

One of the best aspects of these practices is what they foster long term: relationships that defy boundaries. Bootcamp classmates and hackamonth friends will disperse throughout the organization after these programs end, but participants maintain the relationships they forged with each other and with the senior engineers who served as their mentors and coaches. This gives Facebook a cohesiveness and flexibility that's important, as its projects are deeply interconnected. It also gives engineers a view into other parts of the organization and provides them with many more opportunities.

———————

Just as bricks and mortar stores are being undercut by online retailers, so too are many once unstoppable companies now being threatened by new players that rely on new technologies. The video game industry is still going gangbusters, but old-school video game companies like EA and Nintendo stagnated, while Zynga and Rovio (maker of Angry Birds) became some of the hottest companies in the sector. Yahoo!, Flickr, and Shutterfly, which offer online photo sharing platforms, surpassed Kodak, which couldn't stay relevant and eventually filed for bankruptcy, when digital photography and photo sharing replaced film and prints.

What is it that differentiates the successful companies? They offer the world new capability and see the world in a new way. They work on the real-time principles of the Internet, and they embrace the shift to a borderless world, one in which people can work from anywhere and connect on any device. Companies of the future are defined by relationships that are more elastic. We already see young people who are less tolerant of the traditional hierarchies, which are less relevant in organizations that have been flattened by new social technologies. We also see that people want to be entertained. They want to be challenged. They want to work openly and collectively and don't want to be micromanaged. Best of all, they expect and want to be held to a higher standard of contribution.

This is so different from yesterday's way of working, in which companies hoarded employees like limited resources. For the past hundred years, most companies operated from a scarcity mentality, thinking that there was not enough talent, and they did everything possible to try to keep employees within the company walls. Many instituted incentive policies to keep employees in, known as golden handcuffs. Companies devised programs that would pen people in with contracts to keep them for periods of time or vesting schedules that ensured they'd stay, rather than devising ways to make their company the most attractive place to work so that the best talent would flock there—and stay.

But as talent continues to push for change and more companies embrace innovative ways to work, businesses that want to attract and retain their most important asset, their people, will have to leave the antiquated, paternalistic work model behind.

They will have to change how they manage, and move from a command-and-control model to a system driven by meritocracy, empowerment, enhanced freedom—and results.

Many companies have already recognized that consumers are in control. The social web has changed everything about how companies interact with customers. Facebook, Twitter, and other social platforms have given power to the individual in every corner of the world—and taken it away from the corner office, which doesn't exist anymore. Now companies also stand to benefit with more empowered employees. They must transition their focus from commanding, controlling, and owning their employees to retaining top talent and motivating them with freedom and opportunities. All companies can leverage next-generation ideas to change the way we work. For employees and for employers, work is the next killer app.

We have more individuals who want to be entrepreneurs than ever before. It is incumbent upon us to help these folks realize their dreams and ensure that this Age of Entrepreneurship becomes far more powerful and accomplished than the Age of Paternalism. It was a far safer age, but safe generally doesn't lead to greatness.

In the past fifty years, the relationship—and expectations—between workers and employers has completely changed.

The Age of Paternalism Versus the Age of Entrepreneurship

	Age of Paternalism	Age of Entrepreneurship
Length of time someone stays at a job	Twenty-five years to life.	One-and-a-half years.
Length of time companies get "hot"	Greater than five years.	Less than five years.
Length of time companies stay on top	IBM remained the "it" company for twenty-plus years.	Facebook replaced Google as the "it" employer in five years.
Employer's view of employees	Workers work for the company and belong to the company; when employees leave, they are "poached."	Talent is the most valuable asset, but it walks out every night and is on LinkedIn at every moment. Employees opt in; they are not owned.
Turnover	Limited layoffs, turnover low.	Nothing guaranteed either for the company or an employee. Real safety is in skill development and contribution. Company and employee tenure are declining.
Benefits	Pension, health care.	Self-fulfillment, self-direction, freedom.

Conclusion:
Break New Snow

We all have days we remember for the rest of our lives—days that change our perception of everything we are doing and where we are headed. I had such a day the evening I met Mitch Kapor, the founder of Lotus, and one of the greatest thinkers in the technology industry. Mitch had left the companies he had created and was working on his own. He said, "You should come see what I am doing." I enjoyed hearing about his experiences running Kapor Enterprises, working in his family's foundation, doing nonprofit work, helping start-ups, and lending his time to myriad other projects that he found important and inspiring. He stayed in the same place—the place he wanted to live and work from—and took on work that was interesting to him. I realized that this was the model that I wanted. In November 2009, I began to craft what it would look like for me.

With a plan—I used an earlier iteration of the exercise in Chapter Five to articulate it—I was able to start moving toward the life I wanted. In 2011, I resigned as CEO of LiveOps and passed the reins to Marty Beard. I continued to sit on boards I found interesting and where I could make a difference, such as salesforce.com's, and I joined new boards, including Yahoo!'s. I'd been an angel investor for fifteen years—I'd invested in Niku and AdMob, among others—and I created the Webb Investment Network (WIN) to allow me to fuel my passion for working with start-ups and to continue collaborating with friends and past colleagues. My wife and I put a renewed focus on our family's foundation, which is dedicated to helping underprivileged young people gain access to a great education. I wrote this book. I didn't know that writing this book would lead to the founding of a new company, but being open to change enabled this development.

Today I spend my days doing the things that matter to me. I have fewer meetings, but ones with greater impact. I spend more time with my wife and family. As I personally evolved from a company man to become the CEO of my own destiny, I've found it's a lot less safe, but a lot more fulfilling. It's liberating not to have to rely on anyone else, waiting for someone to promote you, notice your work, determine if you are doing good by the company. As the CEO of Your Own Destiny, you are accountable for your own advancement. You'll find great fulfillment in moving out of hope mode and into drive mode.

Ben Franklin famously asked, "Would you rather set goals and achieve everything, or shoot for the stars and fall a little bit short?"

I'd rather shoot for the stars and land in the stratosphere than remain in the status quo. We live in fear of making mistakes, but real growth comes when we are not in our comfort zone. As a society, we are trained to be afraid of failing. On the flip side, we love talking about innovation because it's inherently attached to hope and wrapped in inspiration. I find that curious, because innovation actually carries significant risk. True innovation rests on trying, failing, often pivoting, and trying again. The possibility of failure is perhaps the scariest thing of all, but it also ignites the most spectacular breakthroughs. The results of resilience are nothing short of breathtaking. Thomas Edison failed at forays in mining, construction, and motion pictures, and he discovered hundreds of ways *not* to build a light bulb before he sent electricity around the world. Babe Ruth held a record for strikeouts, not just a record for home runs. Henry Ford had two car companies tank before he created the one that revolutionized modern production. And Sony originally launched with a rice cooker that allegedly burned rice, before the company went on to become an electronics powerhouse.

Although we like to celebrate only the glorious successes, coming to epiphany and innovation also includes a daunting number of upsets. Kathryn Medina was laid off from her job—an unwelcome event, but one that allowed her to move on to something more rewarding by founding her own company and working from where she wanted. The truth is that her previous corporate job didn't provide any more stability than her current one, and yours doesn't either. In March 2012, Apple hit $500 billion in market capitalization, an impressive achievement that only six other companies have hit previously. Interestingly—and demonstrative of how hard it is to stay on top—most of the six are far below that size now.

I hope that this book inspires you to get off the treadmill of your life for a moment and ponder what it is that you really want to achieve. Savor that dream and explore whether you are willing to commit the energy and actions necessary to achieve it. As you think about your career, consider the new world open to you. Work is not confined to the place where you live or to big cities like New York or to fast-growing tech centers like Austin. Work is wherever you want it to be. Today's flexible workforce—for which, I promise you, there is an increasing demand—can work from wherever they want and stay connected via technology and purpose. Of course, as always, the price of this type of flexibility is that you have to perform—this is a system that operates as a meritocracy.

I urge you to seek mentors on the way, but also, and more important, I urge you to serve as a mentor for people you may be able to assist once you have found your way. I have been fortunate to work with individuals who have enlightened me in this area and shown me the power of giving back. At eBay, I saw the power of launching a corporate foundation with pre-IPO stock, as well as the significant impact that Pierre and Pam Omidyar and Jeff Skoll made through their enormous commitment to personal giving, which addresses some of the world's most pressing problems. Marc Benioff took this approach to a new level when he instituted salesforce.com's 1-1-1 integrated philanthropic model (1 percent of employees' time, 1 percent of profit, and 1 percent of company equity go to the community), and his family has made incredible contributions in advancing medicine, including a new world-class children's hospital at the University of California, San Francisco. These leaders have influenced my approach to both corporate and personal philanthropy. They have shown me that we have an obligation to give back more than we receive. They've also shown me how rewarding this can be.

There is so much inspiration and capability in all of us. We could achieve much more individually and as companies if we could unlock the potential that we dream about. And we can do even more if we amplify our impact by helping others reach their aspirations. Finally, we'll find that by giving more, we receive more. We will create a sustainable and better future.

I wanted to write this book and share this with you because as someone who is interested in change, ready for change, and capable of change, you "get it" the most. You will propel this revolution and change the way the world works. You understand the power of technology—and you use the latest tools—to communicate, collaborate, and be more productive. You value time as an asset and don't want to waste it. You care about the environment and don't want to clog our roads with cars, or our atmosphere with pollution. You value common sense over doing something just "because it's always been done that way." I believe that with this mind-set, you will change your life and subsequently change the world of work.

Every season, in every sport, we expect athletes to break new records. We expect players to do everything faster and better. And we're there, cheering them on and excited to see how they will accomplish more than we ever believed imaginable. You have the same opportunity. I wrote this book for you with the hope that you can achieve your dreams, and with the knowledge that it is possible. In doing so, you will revolutionize work and improve the lives of individuals and families for generations to come.

Part 3

Getting Started

Appendix A

The Worksheet

Just what does being the CEO of Your Own Destiny look like? It's different for everyone, but the only way to achieve your goals is to set them. For some, it can be intimidating to set goals that are both aspirational and achievable. Where do you start?

I've come up with a new way, a set of questions that I've used personally and that I've also shared with the employees of eBay and LiveOps.

This worksheet helps you take the pain and frustration out of work and achieve your destiny by encouraging you to identify and articulate where you are and what it is you really want.

Becoming the CEO of Your Own Destiny

Picture yourself on stage in front of work colleagues or people whom you admire the most from your industry. You have the opportunity to tell them your story: all of the challenges, all of the accomplishments, all of the choices you've made. When you are finished, you get to see their reactions. There are only three choices:

A. They are amazed.
B. They think that this is what you should have accomplished.
C. They are unimpressed.

Clearly we know which camp we want them in. But what's the most likely response? Probably B. That's okay. It gives us tools to know what we would like to do differently, and the worksheet below will help you get there.

Take some quiet time by yourself to go through these five steps. They will help you determine what getting to "amazed" means to you. And by helping you articulate what you really want, this process will also serve as the first step in designing a road map to achieving amazing results.

As you go through this exercise, it's important to remember that this is your plan and no one else's. This is a tool intended to help you build a credible and achievable path to your dreams.

1. Aim High

Project yourself five years into the future. You are back in that room on stage. Tell your audience where you are in your life. What has your audience in awe? What would you view as wild success?

_____

_____

_____

If you hear "I can't" when you try to think about your dreams, write down the impediments that you see.

_____

_____

_____

Realize how much is holding you back. Now, consciously let it go.

Start again. Think about what you want. Dream big. Think about your personal and professional lives synergistically. These are not separate dreams. What is your potential, your life purpose? What does success look like to you?

_____

_____

_____

Now, what does success look like in nine months?

_____

_____

_____

In two years?

_____

_____

_____

In five years?

_____

_____

_____

Note: *This Aim High step is not easy.* If truly done well, this will take some energy and soul searching. When you take time to really ponder what YOU want to do, it is very likely to be hard and even uncomfortable. That's okay.

If you are having difficulty articulating clearly what your Aim High goals are, stop and answer the following questions.

- Does combining personal and career goals cause the problem? If so, do the worksheet separately for each and then do the consolidated one.
- Can you articulate Aim High goals in your personal life? If not, think about the things that are holding you back from being able to articulate the goals. Write them down. If your goals are still unclear, you may need to seek some outside coaching or counseling. Dedicating time to talk about these issues will help bring some of the answers to light.

- Can you articulate Aim High goals in your professional life? If not, what questions come into your head that prevent you from achieving clarity? List the questions individually and write down the answers to the best of your ability. If your goals are still unclear, you may need to seek help from a mentor.

The most important aspect of the Aim High exercise is to be totally honest about what you want to achieve. Don't get intimidated by the sacrifices required to achieve your ultimate potential. This section of the worksheet is about your aspirations, not your impediments. (We'll worry about those later.)

2. The Spirit of "And"

What matters most to you in your life? Life is not about pursuing a single purpose. We all have many roles, and we've compartmentalized our work and home lives. People have looked at these as separate spheres. I encourage you to look at them holistically. Here's what most people don't understand: these dual roles do not have to compete. They can coexist and work together, even complement one another. Achieving this, however, requires some planning. You can't have it all with a haphazard approach.

List the different successes that you want to achieve. Be specific. Some examples: ensuring that you are fully available for your children; providing for their college education; being a fully present partner or spouse; achieving economic freedom; having a successful and fulfilling career. The trick here is to recognize what is most important. Prioritize the list.

I want you to dream big. With the advances we've talked about in this book, you can achieve more than ever, but you still need to determine what matters most to you. Even if you've embraced the Spirit of "And," AND you want to do it all, you must recognize that you can't always achieve everything. You must make decisions to determine what's most important so that you can ultimately achieve your goals.

You must always ask the hard question: What trumps what?

Write down your goals as they come to you.

_____

_____

_____

Take time to prioritize them:

1. _____
2. _____
3. _____
4. _____

3. How Can I?

Are there examples, role models, and resources available that illuminate how to achieve your goals? Who else is doing what you want to be doing? What can you learn from them?

List the people you are inspired by who can serve as role models. (You do not have to know them personally.)

_____

_____

_____

Determine how you will figure out their secrets to success or whatever it is you admire most about them. What will you read about them? Is it possible to engage with them?

_____

_____

_____

Given what you've learned, what have you determined your path should be?

_____

_____

_____

4. Do What You Say, Say What You Do

Southwest Airlines CEO Herb Kelleher once said, "We have a strategic plan ... It's called doing things." It's time to do things. It's time to commit to an action plan—one that you can follow.

List three to five things in each of the following categories:

- What will you START doing (that is new and different)?

_____

_____

_____

- What will you STOP doing (that is holding you back from your dreams of success)?

_____

_____

_____

- What will you CONTINUE doing (that you want to take with you on your journey)?

_____

_____

_____

Get feedback from your professional network as well as your personal network (your partner/family/friends) on what you have here.

Take a look at what you've written down and determine whether your outlined actions are credible and, if implemented, will lead to your desired goals. If they are not credible and achievable, iterate accordingly. Now, commit to doing each of these items.

5. Step Back and Reflect

Now that you have gone through this process and gained some perspective, go back and think about your Aim High goals. Do they still resonate with you? Has anything changed?

Success builds on success, so checking in frequently on the goals and readjusting them as you progress are important.

Look at this list every week to determine what you should start, stop, and continue.

Reengage in the process—all five steps—every year.

Examples of completed worksheets are included in Appendix B.

Appendix B

Worksheet Examples

$\mathbf{A}$s I developed this framework for you, I wanted to test its usability and practicality. I filled it out for two times in my career, first when I was entering the workforce and then when I was a midlevel executive in my thirties and facing some career and life challenges. I also have filled it out prospectively for where I am headed now. I share them in the spirit of transparency and also as examples of how dramatically our dreams and aspirations can change over the course of a career.

The first worksheet shows my goals and emotions as I was entering my career.

Personal Worksheet I

1. Aim High

Project yourself five years into the future. You are back in that room on stage. Tell your audience where you are in your life. What has your audience in awe? What would you view as wild success?

A job where I am a manager/leader. I want a new car and eventually a house.

If you hear "I can't" when you try to think about your dreams, write down the impediments that you see.

The best monetary opportunity is in Minnesota, and I live in Florida. I majored in criminal justice.

Realize how much is holding you back. Now, consciously let it go.

Start again. Think about what you want. Dream big. Think about your personal and professional lives synergistically. These are not separate dreams. What is your potential, your life purpose? What does success look like to you?

Being a great provider, being a great employee, becoming a successful independent adult able to do things like take my family on nice vacations, and live in a great neighborhood with great schools

Now, what does success look like in nine months?

A good full-time job and a new car

In two years?

A leadership role en route to a management role, and a house; maybe a child

In five years?

A great career including being a manager, and I've achieved all the things above

2. The Spirit of "And"

Write down your goals as they come to you.

- *Join great company with upward mobility*
- *Have a great job*
- *Be a good husband*
- *Be a good provider*

Take time to prioritize them:

1. *Join great company with upward mobility*
2. *Be a good provider*
3. *Be a good husband*
4. *Have a great job*

3. How Can I?

List the people you are inspired by who can serve as role models. (You do not have to know them personally.)

Friends' parents and my in-laws, who had achieved the success I want

Determine how you will figure out their secrets to success or whatever it is you admire most about them. What will you read about them? Is it possible to engage with them?

I had direct relationships with these people so I was able to probe them: where did they go to school and what did they study, what was their work ethic, what did they see as their accomplishments?

Given what you've learned, what have you determined your path should be?

I wanted to be a successful executive and the first step was making a transition from being a student to becoming a provider with hopes of becoming a manager or leader.

4. Do What You Say, Say What You Do

List three to five things in each of the following categories:

- What will you START doing (that is new and different)?
  a. *Move to Minnesota*
  b. *Take an entry-level security job*
  c. *Do a great job*
- What you will STOP doing (that is holding you back from your dreams of success)?
  a. *Going to school*
  b. *Living in Florida*
  c. *Working traditional daytime schedule*
- What you will CONTINUE doing (that you want to take with you on your journey)?
  a. *Being motivated/high achiever/learner*
  b. *Being family oriented*
  c. *Adhering to my value system*

5. Step Back and Reflect

Now that you have gone through this process and have some perspective, go back and think about your Aim High goals. Do they still resonate with you? Has anything changed?

Upon reflection, my career took off. However, my personal life struggled.

The following worksheet was filled out for a different point in my life, when I was around thirty-eight and a director of IT at Quantum. My wife, Irene, was a finance manager at Quantum. I had four kids, two from my first marriage and two from my second marriage. With our dual incomes, we were able to handle child support and live a nice life with our kids. My children ranged from four to fourteen years old. When our youngest was three, we almost lost her to *E. coli*. Irene decided she definitely wanted to stay home and raise the kids, but we didn't know if we could swing it financially.

Personal Worksheet II

1. Aim High

Project yourself five years into the future. You are back in that room on stage. Tell your audience where you are in your life. What has your audience in awe? What would you view as wild success?

I need to provide economics to let Irene be a full-time mother for my younger two kids, and I must still provide appropriately for the whole family. I want to be a top IT executive at a major technology company. I want to be respected enough to also serve on a board of directors. I must ensure that all kids can go to great colleges and that we have earned enough to retire by our mid-50s.

If you hear "I can't" when you try to think about your dreams, write down the impediments that you see.

- *Economics don't work and we'll be using savings potentially.*
- *We'll have to cut way back on things we've been accustomed to.*

- *While I am doing well, I'm not clear that my current career trajectory can be vectored to meet the goals.*
- *Do Irene and I have a great relationship without work in it? (We've worked together at the same companies all through our marriage.)*
- *I am going to have to work even harder.*

Realize how much is holding you back. Now, consciously let it go.

Start again. Think about what you want. Dream big. Think about your personal and professional lives synergistically. These are not separate dreams. What is your potential, your life purpose? What does success look like to you?

Now, what does success look like in nine months?

- *Back to at least break even on one salary*
- *Making career progress on my IT dreams*
- *The younger kids, Irene, and I are all blossoming*

In two years?

- *Promoted into a better technology CIO job*
- *Start doing advisory work*
- *Be significantly adding to net worth of family*
- *Family unit stays strong and is progressing*

In five years?

- *Be viewed as one of the top CIOs in the country*
- *Be on boards of directors*
- *Family unit stays strong and is progressing*
- *Clearly on way to economic dreams*

2. The Spirit of "And"

Write down your goals as they come to you.

- *Ensure kids have Irene to take care of them full-time*
- *Provide economically for all the family near term and in the future*
- *Family unit stays strong and progressing*
- *Keep intellectually stimulated*
- *Career progression*

Take time to prioritize them:

1. *Irene at home with kids*
2. *Career progression*
3. *Provide economically for all the family*
4. *Family unit strong*
5. *Intellectual stimulation*

3. How Can I?

List the people you are inspired by who can serve as role models. (You do not have to know them personally.)

Leading CIOs at companies such as AT&T, FedEx, Charles Schwab, and Sun Microsystems. CEOs at high tech companies, including Apple, HP, and Microsoft. Leaders at companies with great cultures like GE.

Determine how you will figure out their secrets to success or whatever it is you admire most about them. What will you read about them? Is it possible to engage with them?

I identified and researched CIOs and created a database of them. I went to events where leaders I admired were speaking and over time built relationships with them.

Given what you've learned, what have you determined your path should be?

Develop a database of killer CIOs and figure out what my secret sauce is going to be. Look into networking beyond my company to understand how advisory roles happened and also what is involved in board of director roles.

4. Do What You Say, Say What You Do

- What will you START doing (that is new and different)?
  a. *Appreciating how blessed the kids were to have Irene's full-time focus*
  b. *Working even harder and making more money sooner*
  c. *Building an even stronger relationship with Irene without work in it*
- What will you STOP doing (that is holding you back from your dreams of success)?
  a. *Spending money as though we had two incomes*

    b. *Having to worry about childcare*
    c. *Dreaming about getting to big jobs—now I must deliver on those dreams and get to great jobs*
    d. *Viewing myself as a bit of an underdog*
- What will you CONTINUE doing (that you want to take with you on your journey)?
    a. *Value system*
    b. *Work ethic and results*
    c. *Family orientation*

5. Step Back and Reflect

Now that you have gone through this process and gained some perspective, go back and think about your Aim High goals. Do they still resonate with you? Has anything changed?

I made all of it happen, but it wasn't without sacrifice on all fronts.

    The third personal worksheet, below, I filled out when I was stepping down from the CEO position at LiveOps and pursuing a new phase of life.

Personal Worksheet III

1. Aim High

Project yourself five years into the future. You are back in that room on stage. Tell your audience where you are in your life. What has your audience in awe? What would you view as wild success?

Be a soul mate to Irene and be a fabulous family member to my family. Ensure that we go everywhere and see everything that we desire. Stay healthy and active. Celebrate our 50th wedding anniversary in style! Helping identify, grow, and/or mentor 2–5 next-generation transformational companies in technology. Provide a path for high-tech executives to amplify their personal impact in the world. Give back through the Webb Family Foundation in a dramatic and high-impact fashion.

If you hear "I can't" when you try to think about your dreams, write down the impediments that you see.

- *How can I stay healthy—it is not totally in my control*
- *How will I find one transformational company—let alone 2–5?*
- *Driving impact through philanthropy is hard to measure—what do I mean by dramatic?*

Realize how much is holding you back. Now, consciously let it go.

Start again. Think about what you want. Dream big. Think about your personal and professional lives synergistically. These are not separate dreams. What is your potential, your life purpose? What does success look like to you?

This has changed over the years pretty radically. Originally it was to provide for my family in a way that my father was unable to for us. As I met Irene, my purpose was to experience a long-lasting, growing, loving marriage and raise great kids. Now it is about enjoying my personal life to the fullest with Irene and family, while coaching and mentoring others in big and dramatic ways. Get the best of both worlds—great family time and great world impact.

Now, what does success look like in nine months?

- *Totally out of any full-time operating role.*
- *Webb Investment Network (WIN) in full swing, with point of view about which space/area we want to focus on for one of the transformational companies we're working with.*
- *Webb Family Foundation (WFF) has a great year, and family is fully engaged and satisfied with progress.*
- *We have taken the first of our special trips post work (probably swing through the family in US) and have two+ additional trips planned for the year.*

In two years?

- *Still enjoying the great family time and great world impact.*
- *Have seen at least one positive exit in WIN.*
- *WIN runs without much direct involvement and continues to be high energy and fun for all.*
- *We have become engaged with at least one company that we think will be truly transformational.*
- *WFF is really humming, and we know that our donations are having great impact.*

In five years?

- *Still enjoying the great family time and great world impact.*
- *Have been to all the original list of places we wanted to visit in our lifetime.*
- *We have experienced great returns from WIN and believe we are vectored to a 3X overall return for the investments.*
- *We have one confirmed transformational company and two engagements that could be transformational.*
- *WFF has grown over 50%, and the impact from our donations has grown even faster.*

2. The Spirit of "And"

Write down your goals as they come to you.

- *Get out of operating role*
- *More and better quality time with Irene*
- *Stay healthy and in shape*
- *WIN running smoothly and without much direct help from me*
- *WFF growing and having an impact*
- *Identifying and participating in transformational companies*

Take time to prioritize them:

1. *Get out of operating role*
2. *More and better quality time with Irene*
3. *Stay healthy and in shape*
4. *Identifying and participating in transformational companies*
5. *WIN running smoothly*
6. *WFF growing and having an impact*

3. How Can I?

List the people you are inspired by who can serve as role models. (You do not have to know them personally.)

Marc Benioff, Bill Gates, Pierre Omidiyar, and Jeff Skoll are great inspirational role models for how we may lead our foundation. There are many angel network models to learn from—for example, Jeff Clavier, Ron Conway, and Mike Maples. I will have to model more people who have transitioned effectively to become the CEO of Their Own Destiny like Mitch Kapor. For the next 10 years, I totally want to keep having major impact while having more time to enjoy my wife and family.

Determine how you will figure out their secrets to success or whatever it is you admire most about them. What will you read about them? Is it possible to engage with them?

In most cases, these are people I have a relationship with. In some cases I need to develop and build better relationships with some of the angel network executives, which I will do.

Given what you've learned, what have you determined your path should be?

Becoming the CEO of my own destiny: getting the intellectual stimulation I desire while making an impact on the world, yet having much more time with my loved ones.

4. Do What You Say, Say What You Do

- What will you START doing (that is new and different)?
  a. *Identifying the must-dos for Irene and me over the next 5 years*
  b. *Spending more time with Irene and family*
  c. *Finding even better deals for WIN and pushing it to operate without me*
- What will you STOP doing (that is holding you back from your dreams of success)?
  a. *Holding down an operating role*
  b. *Feeling the need to join an organization*
- What will you CONTINUE doing (that you want to take with you on your journey)?
  a. *Making progress on WIN and WFF*
  b. *Engaging experiences with family members*
  c. *Striving for world impact*

5. Step Back and Reflect

Now that you have gone through this process and gained some perspective, go back and think about your Aim High goals. Do they still resonate with you? Has anything changed?

Stay tuned . . .

Appendix C

Services You Should Know About

The number of free productivity tools on the market is exploding. We use many of these tools at WIN and have been able to reduce costs and increase flexibility.

File Management and Storage. Cloud-based tools like Dropbox, Box.net, and AeroFS (disclosure: I am an investor in this company) make it easy to quickly and easily share documents while preserving the file system organization.

Document Collaboration and Sharing. Tools like Dropbox are great for sharing completed files (for example, final presentations), but they are not necessarily the most effective means of collaborating on simple documents like spreadsheets, to-do lists, or notes. Here is a list of the tools we use at WIN to manage our team, track our progress, and collaborate on projects like travel plans or simple budgets.

- **Smartsheet.** A very simple and easy-to-program spreadsheet in the cloud. We use Smartsheet for a number of purposes, and many of the sheets serve as "master copies" of the documents and lists we use every day. Our mailing lists, for example, are maintained in Smartsheet, as are our weekly task lists and our quarterly objectives.

- **Google Docs.** Very similar in functionality to Smartsheet, but as it is a suite, it includes other tools, such as word processing and presentation creation. Also of note, **Google Apps** offers free email and calendaring on your own domain name.
- **Evernote.** Note-taking in the cloud. Evernote makes it easy to sync your notes across your computer, laptop, and mobile devices. This service is particularly useful for quickly pulling notes from earlier meetings on to a smartphone or iPad while on the go.
- **Pivotal Tracker.** A free project management tool perfectly suited to managing development features for a small team.

Meeting Remotely. Thanks to ever-increasing bandwidth speeds (and the parallel drop in cost), there are number of low-cost (or in some cases free) tools that enable teams to meet remotely. Working from home was never as much of a possibility as it is today. Ranging from conference call solutions to video-chat solutions, here is a collection of the tools we use regularly:

- **GoToMeeting.** Easily schedule conference calls for domestic and international participants. Can use a standard phone and dial-in process or VoIP through the computer and a microphone.
- **WebEx or join.me.** Marries conference calling with document and screen sharing. These are popular options with start-ups during the pitch process.

- **Skype.** One of the most popular solutions for placing inexpensive (or free when using Skype-to-Skype) calls. Many companies in our portfolio also use Skype to hold video check-ins with their distributed teams.

Electronic Signatures. As an investment entity, WIN has to send and receive executed, signed documents on a regular and frequent basis. The rise of easy-to-use electronic signature services is quickly making the fax machine a tool of the past.

- HelloFax/HelloSign
- DocuSign
- eFax

News. Tools to organize, store, and share news are crucial to staying current and avoiding getting lost in the flood. The following are some of the current tools we use at WIN to surface, organize, store, and share articles.

- **Yahoo! News and Finance.** A very simple way to stay abreast of any new content on the web, which matches preset keyword criteria.
- **Google Alerts.** At WIN, we use Google Alerts to monitor the Internet for mentions of our name or the names of our portfolio companies.
- **Google Reader.** My colleagues use an RSS reader, such as Google's offering, to subscribe to key media outlets (such as TechCrunch), star the articles they find interesting, and share these articles with the rest of the team. Although it may take some time up front to set up your RSS feeds, in the long run this solution can be much more effective than

copying and pasting entire articles or links for storage and sharing.

- **Pulse** and **Flipboard.** We use these iOS and Android applications to access our RSS feeds in a beautiful and intuitive user interface while on our mobile devices.
- **Instapaper** or **Pocket.** Do you ever have the problem wherein someone sends you an article over email (or mentions it in conversation) and you want to read it eventually, but are concerned that you will forget about it or misplace the link? These services help create a reading list of any saved articles and can be accessed on mobile devices. Simply create an account and save articles to your list using the provided browser plug-in.

Notes

Introduction

1. Rebecca L. Ray and Thomas Rizzacasa, *Job Satisfaction: 2012 Edition*, Conference Board (June 2012), http://www.conference-board.org/publications /publicationdetail.cfm?publicationid=2258; AP, "Poll: Most in US Don't Like Their Jobs," *New York Post*, January 5, 2010, http://www.nypost.com/p /news/business/poll_most_in_us_don_like_their_jobs_4iRFvxrVqLk3mxt MVmCULO#ixzz1pDBNzVQL.

2. Gail Marks Jarvis, "Employee Moral Ebbs Along with Workforce," *Chicago Tribune*, July 1, 2011, http://articles.chicagotribune.com/2011-07 -01/features/sc-cons-0630-marksjarvis-20110701_1_employers-workforce -mercer; source information from Mercer, *Inside Employees' Minds: Navigating the New Rules of Engagement (US Survey Summary)* (June 2011), http://inside -employees-mind.mercer.com/flash/mercer-pkg/download_US.html.

3. Susie Steiner, "Top Five Regrets of the Dying," *Guardian*, February 12, 2012, http://www.guardian.co.uk/lifeandstyle/2012/feb/01/top-five-regrets -of-the-dying.

4. Sara Horowitz, "Revolution of Our Time," *Atlantic*, September 1, 2011, http://www.theatlantic.com/business/archive/2011/09/the-freelance-surge -is-the-industrial-revolution-of-our-time/244229/#.TmALomZt5E4.email.

5. NCAA, "Estimated Probability of Competing in Athletics Beyond the High School Interscholastic Level" (September 27, 2011), http://www.ncaa.org /wps/wcm/connect/public/ncaa/pdfs/2011/2011+probability+of+going+pro.

Chapter 1

1. George Friedman, *The Next 100 Years* (New York: Doubleday, 2009).

2. CareerBuilder and *USA Today*, "Mid-Year Job Forecast 2010" (July 1, 2010), http://viewer.zmags.com/publication/2d473322#/2d473322/1.

3. Steven F. Hipple, "Self-Employment in the United States," *Monthly Labor Review*, September 2010, 22–23, http://www.bls.gov/opub/mlr/2010/09 /art2full.pdf.

4. Ilana Kowarski, "Freelance Jobs: Half of All New Jobs in Recovery?" *Christian Science Monitor*, June 13, 2011, http://www.csmonitor.com/Business /2011/0613/Freelance-jobs-Half-of-all-new-jobs-in-recovery.

5. U.S. Government Accountability Office, "Employment Arrangements: Improved Outreach Could Help Ensure Proper Worker Classification" (GAO, July 2006), http://www.gao.gov/new.items/d06656.pdf; Anita Creamer, "Freelancers Create Jobs for Themselves," *Sacramento Bee*, May 11, 2010, http://guide.sacbee.com/2010/05/23/4093/freelancers.html.

6. Horowitz quoted in Creamer, "Freelancers Create Jobs for Themselves."

7. U.S. Green Building Council, "Building Design Leaders Collaborating on Carbon-Neutral Buildings by 2030" (May 7, 2007), http://www.usgbc.org /News/PressReleaseDetails.aspx?ID=3124.

8. U.S. Department of Transportation, Office of Operations, "Operations— Did You Know?—Archive" (July 14, 2012), http://ops.fhwa.dot.gov /resources/didyouknow/didyouknow_archive.asp.

9. U.S. General Services Administration, "Workspace Utilization and Allocation Benchmark" (July 2011): 20, http://www.gsa.gov/portal/content /105262.

10. Ibid., 19.

11. Ibid., 19; Maureen Sirhall, "Agency Sees Gains from Telework Initiative," *Government Executive*, April 15, 2003. Retrieved from http://webcache .googleusercontent.com/search?q=cache:gZiJ60xo-acJ:www.govexec.com /pay-benefits/2003/04/agency-sees-gains-from-telework-initiative/13870 /+&cd=1&hl=en&ct=clnk&gl=us.

12. U.S. General Services Administration, "Workspace Utilization," 17.

13. Ibid, 33.

Chapter 2

1. Marc Andreessen, "Why Software Is Eating the World," *Wall Street Journal*, August 20, 2011, http://online.wsj.com/article/SB10001424053111903480904576512250915629460.html.

2. Michio Kaku, *Physics of the Future* (New York: Knopf Doubleday, 2011), 21.

3. Giselle Tsirulnik, "Mary Meeker: Mobile Driving Most Dramatic Behavior Transformation in History," *Mobile Marketer*, February 11, 2011, http://www.mobilemarketer.com/cms/news/advertising/9052.html. Video of the presentation can be found at http://www.youtube.com/watch?v=sZO9e1wV23U#t=09m58s.

4. Andreessen, "Why Software Is Eating the World."

5. Cory A. Booker, "5th Annual State of the City Address 2011" (2011), http://www.ci.newark.nj.us/userimages/downloads/mayor_SOTC2011 Transcript.pdf.

Chapter 3

1. Tara Siegel Bernard, "As Dewey Collapses, Partners and Retirees Face Big Financial Losses," *New York Times*, May 11, 2012, B1.

Chapter 4

1. Gary Hamel, *What Matters Now* (San Francisco: Jossey-Bass, 2012).

2. Ibid.

3. Rudi Volti, *An Introduction to the Sociology of Work and Occupations* (Thousand Oaks, CA: Pine Forge Press, 2008), 32; Razor Suleman (Achievers), "R.I.P. Traditional Service Awards: Long Live Recognition Milestones" (white paper), 2, http://www.achievers.com/sites/default/files/achievers -whitepaper-rip-traditional-service-awards.pdf.

4. Suleman, "R.I.P. Traditional Service Awards."

5. Daniel Jacoby, *Laboring for Freedom: A New Look at the History of Labor in America* (Armonk, NY: M. E. Sharpe, 1998), 92; Roland Marchand, *Creating the Corporate Soul: The Rise of Public Relations and Corporate Imagery in American Big Business* (Berkeley: University of California Press, 2001), 115.

6. Robert Whaples, "Hours of Work in U.S. History," EH.net, February 1, 2010, http://eh.net/encyclopedia/article/whaples.work.hours.us.

7. Levinson cited in Craig E. Aronoff and John L. Ward, "The High Cost of Paternalism," *Nation's Business* 81, no. 5 (May 1993): 61; see also Harry Levinson, "Reciprocation: The Relationship Between Man and Organization," *Administrative Science Quarterly* 9, no. 4 (March 1965): 381–382.

8. U.S. Department of Labor, "National Compensation Survey: Employee Benefits in Private Industry in the United States, March 2007" (August 2007): 9, http://www.bls.gov/ncs/ebs/sp/ebsm0006.pdf; Emily Brandon, "Jobs That Still Offer Traditional Pensions," *US News and World Report*, June 1, 2009, http://money.usnews.com/money/retirement/articles/2009/06/01/jobs-that-still-offer-traditional-pensions.

9. Brandon, "Jobs That Still Offer Traditional Pensions"; Pension Rights Center, "Companies That Have Changed Their Defined Benefit Pension Plans," http://www.pensionrights.org/publications/fact-sheet/companies-have-changed-their-defined-benefit-pension-plans.

10. Brandon, "Jobs That Still Offer Traditional Pensions"; Towers Watson, "Press Releases: Majority of Fortune 100 Companies Offer Only Defined Contribution Plans to New Salaried Employees, Watson Wyatt Analysis Finds" (May 11, 2009), http://www.watsonwyatt.com/render.asp?catid=1&id=21177.

11. Henry Farber, "Is the Company Man an Anachronism?" Working Paper no. 518, Princeton University Industrial Relations Section (2007), 1.

12. Ibid.

13. Suleman, "R.I.P. Traditional Service Awards," 3.

14. Jeff Daugherty, "Pitfalls of a Paternalistic Management Style," CFS Group's Blog, posted March 5, 2010, http://jeffdaugherty.wordpress.com/2010/03/05/pitfalls-of-a-paternalistic-management-style/.

15. "Running Faster, Falling Behind: John Hagel III on How American Business Can Catch Up," *Knowledge@Wharton*, June 23, 2010, http://knowledge.wharton.upenn.edu/article.cfm?articleid=2523.

16. Allan Engelhardt, "The 3/2 rule of employee productivity," *CYBAEA Journal*, October 16, 2006, http://www.cybaea.net/Blogs/Journal/employee_productivity.html.

17. WorldatWork, "Telework Trendlines" (2009), http://www.worldatwork.org/waw/adimLink?id=31115.

18. Michael Malone, *The Future Arrived Yesterday* (New York: Crown Business, 2009).

19. John Hagel III, John Seely Brown, and Duleesha Kulasooriya, *The 2011 Shift Index* (2011): 24–25, 98, http://www.deloitte.com/assets/Dcom-United States/Local%20Assets/Documents/us_tmt_2011shiftindex_111011.pdf.

20. U.S. General Services Administration, "Workspace Utilization and Allocation Benchmark" (July 2011): 17, http://www.gsa.gov/portal/content /105262.

21. Mario Toneguzzi, "Tech Pioneer Champions Calgary Telework Initiative," *Calgary Herald*, April 23, 2010, http://www2.canada.com/calgaryherald /news/calgarybusiness/story.html?id=4b9c6ceb-29c9-4df5-896a -567c5fe5a6d1.

22. All examples cited in this paragraph are from company materials from Better Workplace (http://www.betterworkplace.com) or from an interview with Ian Gover, Better Workplace CEO.

23. Kate Lister and Tom Harnish, "Workshifting Benefits: The Bottom Line," Telework Research Network (prepared for Citrix Online) (May 2010): 6, http://www.workshifting.com/downloads/downloads/Workshifting%20 Benefits-The%20Bottom%20Line.pdf.

Chapter 5

1. John Hagel III, John Seely Brown, and Duleesha Kulasooriya, *The 2009 Shift Index* (2009), http://www.scribd.com/doc/24183753/Deloitte-Center -for-the-Edge-Shift-Index-Industry-Perspectives-by-John-Hagel-John -Seely-Brown-and-Lang-Davison.

2. Robert Whaples, "Hours of Work in U.S. History," EH.net, February 1, 2010, http://eh.net/encyclopedia/article/whaples.work.hours.us.

3. Sylvia Ann Hewlett and Lauren Leader-Chivée with Catherine Fredman, Maggie Jackson, and Laura Sherbin, "The X Factor: Tapping into the Strengths of the 33- to 46-Year-Old Generation," Center for Work-Life Policy Study sponsored by American Express, Boehringer Ingelheim USA, Cisco, Credit Suisse, and Google (September 2011), https://www .worklifepolicy.org/documents/X%20Factor%20Press%20Release%20 final.pdf.

4. Rachel Emma Silverman, "Looking for Ideas in Shared Workspaces," *Wall Street Journal*, March 20, 2012, http://online.wsj.com/article/SB1000142405 2702303812904577293853649106414.html; see also Carl King, "Profiling Coworkers in the United States" (February 1, 2011), http://www .deskmag.com/en/coworker-profile-usa-coworking-175.

Chapter 6

1. Steven Sauter et al., "Stress . . . at Work," National Institute for Occupational Health and Safety Working Paper No. 99–101 (1999), http://www.cdc.gov/niosh/docs/99-101/pdfs/99-101.pdf; see also Column Five, "Desk Rage: The Tell-Tale Signs of an Overworked Employee," infographic on *Alltop*, posted May 21, 2012, http://holykaw.alltop.com/desk -rage-the-tell-tale-signs-of-an-overworke?tu2=1.

2. American Institute of Stress, "Attitudes in the American Workplace VII" (June 2001), http://americaninstituteofstress.org/wp-content/uploads /2011/08/2001Attitude-in-the-Workplace-Harris.pdf.

3. Jonah Lehrer, "Your Co-Workers Might Be Killing You: Hours Don't Affect Health Much—but Unsupportive Colleagues Do," *Wall Street Journal*, August 20, 2011, http://online.wsj.com/article/SB10001424053111903 3929045765122331165763552.html.

4. Ibid.

5. Catherine Rampell, "The Self-Employed Are the Happiest," *New York Times*, September 16, 2009, http://economix.blogs.nytimes.com/2009/09 /16/the-self-employed-are-the-happiest/.

6. Matthias Benz and Bruno S. Frey, "Being Independent Is a Great Thing: Subjective Evaluations of Self-Employment and Hierarchy," *Economica* 75 (2008): 362; Will Wilkinson, "Happiness, Freedom, and Autonomy," *Forbes*, March 23, 2011, http://www.forbes.com/sites/willwilkinson/2011 /03/23/happiness-and-freedom/.

7. Wilkinson, "Happiness, Freedom, and Autonomy."

8. Paolo Verme, "Happiness, Freedom and Control," Università Commerciale Luigi Bocconi, Econpubblica Centre for Research on the Public Sector, Working Paper No. 141 (July 3, 2009); available at SSRN: http://ssrn.com /abstract=1499652; Wilkinson, "Happiness, Freedom, and Autonomy."

9. CCH, "2007 Unscheduled Absence Survey" (October, 10 2007), http://www.cch.com/press/news/2007/20071010h.asp.

10. Kate Lister and Tom Harnish, "Workshifting Benefits: The Bottom Line," Telework Research Network (prepared for Citrix Online) (May 2010), http://www.workshifting.com/downloads/downloads/Workshifting%20Benefits-The%20Bottom%20Line.pdf.

11. Atul Gwande, "Personal Best," New Yorker, October 3, 2011, http://www.newyorker.com/reporting/2011/10/03/111003fa_fact_gawande#ixzz1kU5yz5S2.

12. Jim Billington, "Meet Your New Mentor. It's a Network," Harvard Business Review, August 1, 1997, 3. Available at http://hbr.org/product/meet-your-new-mentor-it-s-a-network/an/U9708A-PDF-ENG.

13. Matt Marx, "The Firm Strikes Back: Non-Compete Agreements and the Mobility of Technical Professionals," American Sociological Review. 76, no. 5 (October 2011): 695–712.

14. Ross Jones, "Measuring the Success of Coaching and Mentoring," Human Capital Institute white paper (May 18, 2007): 3, http://www.menttium.com/servlet/servlet.FileDownload?file=00P80000007kxTsEAI.

15. For an overview of this research, please see Tammy D. Allen, Lillian T. Eby, Mark L. Poteet, Elizabeth Lentz, and Lizzette Lima, "Career Benefits Associated with Mentoring for Protégés: A Meta-Analysis," Journal of Applied Psychology 89, no. 1 (February 2004): 127–136.

16. Monica C. Higgins and Kathy E. Kram, "Reconceptualizing Mentoring at Work: A Developmental Network Perspective," Academy of Management Review 26, no. 2 (April 2001): 264–288.

17. Sheryl Branch, "The 100 Best Companies to Work for in America," Fortune 139, no. 1 (1999): 118–130.

18. Jacque Wilson, "Want to Lose Weight? Shut Your Mouth," CNN, November 14, 2011, http://www.cnn.com/2011/11/14/health/lose-weight-mouth-shut-secret/index.html. For additional research on goal setting, see Peter M. Gollwitzer, Paschal Sheeran, Verena Michalski, and Andrea E. Seifert, "When Intentions Go Public: Does Social Reality Widen the Intention-Behavior Gap?" Psychological Science 20, no. 5 (2009): 612–618.

19. Billington, "Meet Your New Mentor. It's a Network," 4.

20. Jonathan Spira and Joshua Feintuch, *The Cost of Not Paying Attention: How Interruptions Impact Knowledge Worker Productivity* (Basex, September 2005): 4, http://www.basex.com/web/tbghome.nsf/23e5e39594c064ee852564ae 004fa010/ea4eae828bd411be8525742f0006cde3/$file/costofnotpaying attention.basexreport.pdf; Lister and Harnish, "Workshifting Benefits."

Chapter 7

1. Paul D. Reynolds, "Who Starts New Firms? Preliminary Explorations of Firms-in-Gestation," *Small Business Economics* 9, no. 5 (October 1997): 449–462.

2. Sylvia Ann Hewlett and Lauren Leader-Chivée with Catherine Fredman, Maggie Jackson, and Laura Sherbin, "The X Factor: Tapping into the Strengths of the 33- to 46-Year-Old Generation," Center for Work-Life Policy Study sponsored by American Express, Boehringer Ingelheim USA, Cisco, Credit Suisse, and Google (September 2011), https://www .worklifepolicy.org/documents/X%20Factor%20Press%20Release%20 final.pdf.

3. Kevin Lincoln, "At Stanford, If You Haven't Started a Company by Graduation, You're a Failure," *Business Insider*, September 20, 2011, http://www .businessinsider.com/stanford-startup-culture-2011-9.

4. John A. Byrne, "MBA Startups at Stanford Reach All-Time High," *Fortune*, June 1, 2012, http://management.fortune.cnn.com/2012/06/01/mba -startups-stanford/.

5. Ibid.

6. Jocelyn Lincoln and Megan M. Raferty, "Free Agents: How 'Knowledge Workers' Are Redefining the Workplace," Kelly Outsourcing & Consulting Group white paper (2011): 9; available at http://www.kellyocg.com /Knowledge/White_Papers/Free_Agents_-_How_Knowledge_Workers _are_Redefining_the_Workplace/.

7. Scott Shane, "Why Do Most Start Ups Fail?" *Small Business Trends*, September 26, 2011, http://smallbiztrends.com/2011/09/why-do-most-start-ups -fail.html. For more information, see Small Business Association, "Frequently Asked Questions" (updated January 2011), http://www.sba .gov/sites/default/files/sbfaq.pdf and Bureau of Labor Statistics, "Survival

of Private Sector Establishments by Opening Year," http://www.bls.gov/bdm/us_age_naics_00_table7.txt.

8. Dane Stangler, "High Growth Firms and the Future of the American Economy," Kaufman Foundation Research Series (March 2012): 7–8, http://www.kauffman.org/uploadedfiles/high-growth-firms-study.pdf.

9. Carmen Noble, "Why Companies Fail—and How Their Founders Can Bounce Back," *HBS Working Knowledge*, March 7, 2011, 1.

10. Ben Horowitz, "Building a Technology Company," A. Richard Newton Distinguished Innovator Lecture Series Presentation at University of California Berkeley (November 3, 2009), http://www.youtube.com/watch?v=1GTbAI_2yh4.

11. Ben Horowitz, "Picking a General Partner," ben's blog, posted March 1, 2011, http://bhorowitz.com/2011/03/01/picking-a-general-partner/.

12. Alyson Shontell, "Meet Ben Silbermann, the Brilliant Young Co-Founder of Pinterest," *Business Insider*, March 13, 2012, http://articles.businessinsider.com/2012-03-13/tech/31158694_1_google-experience-products-silbermann-said#ixzz1vpOjLiOi.

13. Ibid.

14. Ibid.

15. Arden Pennell, "Want to Have an Exit Like Instagram? Here's Something Every Founder Needs to Know," *Business Insider*, April 9, 2012, http://articles.businessinsider.com/2012-04-09/news/31311235_1_founders-andreessen-horowitz-product-entrepreneurs.

16. Chris Dixon, "When Should You Give Up on an Idea?" (May 24, 2012), http://cdixon.org/2012/05/24/when-should-you-give-up-on-an-idea/.

17. Shane, "Why Do Most Start Ups Fail?"

Chapter 8

1. David Card, "Supporting Millennials in the Enterprise," *gigaOM*, August 22, 2011, http://gigaom.com/2011/08/22/supporting-millennials-in-the-enterprise/.

2. Razor Suleman (Achievers), "R.I.P. Traditional Service Awards: Long Live Recognition Milestones" (white paper), 3–5, http://www.achievers.com/sites/default/files/achievers-whitepaper-rip-traditional-service-awards.pdf.

Acknowledgments

First, thank you for letting me share my beliefs and passions with you. I know how many demands there are on everyone's time these days, so I am deeply appreciative of the time you have spent with me.

I'm grateful to many people for helping with this book. My partner in writing the book, Carlye Adler, was fabulous. She made the whole project fun and inspiring. She was always able—in a very nice way—to prod me into iterating on points until the essence of the point became clear. My wife, Irene, and son Kevin read every chapter (many times), provided great input, and were supporters throughout. My partner at work, Dena Porter, was subjected to many a quick proofread and edit, and always provided valuable insight. Jeremy Schneider was a very, very important and integral part of the team and a tireless and enthusiastic researcher and proofreader; his integrity as well as his hard work, dedication, and intrepid reporting made this book better, and I am deeply indebted. Kristin Wahl, formerly at LiveOps, was supportive of the book from the beginning and helped us get started. Marie Jackson, the former LiveOps CMO, participated heavily in the book, and her contributions are many. I appreciate the editing help from current LiveOps CMO, Ann Ruckstuhl. Michael Neril and Michael Bergelson provided constructive input throughout the writing process. Henry Gomez at Hewlett-Packard is responsible for advancing the book's foreword from a request to a reality. I'm indebted to Karen Murphy of Jossey-Bass for her support, her partnership, and for leading a fantastic editing process. I'm grateful to Mary Garrett, Mark Karmendy, Michele Jones, and the Jossey-Bass team for making this book something of which we all are proud.

There have been many people who have had a huge impact on my learnings from the work world. I want to recognize a few of my bosses and mentors from my career: Dick Mainey, John Martone, and Ed Marill from IBM (you guys saw more in me than I saw in myself); John Frandsen and Walt Thirion from Thomas-Conrad for letting me become a product executive when I had no background in it; Pierre Patkay and Michael Brown for taking a huge chance on me at Quantum as an unknown IT leader; Bill Ruehle and Andy Ludwick for giving me a chance to spread my CIO wings at Bay Networks; Ted Waitt and Jeff Weitzen for the great opportunity at Gateway; Meg Whitman and Pierre Omidyar for providing me with the career ride of my life at eBay, first as president of technology, then as COO; Bill Trenchard, Doug Carlisle, and Bill Gurley for the CEO opportunity at LiveOps; and the great entrepreneur Mitch Kapor for inspiring me to truly become the CEO of my own destiny and pursue what matters to me most.

I was very inspired by all the independent home agents at LiveOps and the employees, all of whom truly get the monumental shift that is under way and who are changing the world of work every day.

I also thank a few of the CEOs with whom I have had the privilege to work as a board member: Marc Benioff at salesforce.com, Omar Hamoui at AdMob, Godfrey Sullivan at Hyperion, Marty Beard at LiveOps, Marissa Mayer at Yahoo!, and Michael Fleisher and Gene Hall at Gartner.

I also know that the only way to make things happen in any job are with the help of good people. I have been blessed with some extraordinary talent on my teams and among my peers. I am grateful that several of them are still working with me as affiliates of the Webb Investment Network (WIN). In this iteration of my career, I am always humbled and astonished by all the young and passionate entrepreneurs whom we have the opportunity to invest in and watch grow at WIN. I also thank Adriane Glazier, the founding director for the Webb Family Foundation, for getting our foundation off the ground, and Han Hong for leading it into its next phase.

Finally, I thank my family. Everything I have accomplished in my life is directly related to their impact on me. My mother, Helen, set an unbelievable example of how not to let life beat you down. My only brother, Tony, was willing to constantly coach and encourage his much younger brother to aim high. My sisters, Lynne, Helen, and Edna, all had a significant impact on me.

My children, Carrie; Mitchell and his wife, Kaley; and Kevin and Laura have challenged me, inspired me, and continue to bring me hope every day. I am blessed to have grandchildren, and I hope that someday they will become the CEOs of their own destinies.

Irene, you are the love of my life and my best friend. There is no way I would have completed this book or anything in my career without your constant and deep support. You inspire me in so many ways and you have taught me so much about love and family. I am forever indebted to you.

About the Authors

Maynard Webb is a thirty-year veteran of the technology industry. An active leader in the technology and business community, Webb serves as a board member, investor, philanthropist, and mentor to young entrepreneurs.

As the founder of the Webb Investment Network (WIN), a seed investment firm dedicated to nurturing entrepreneurs, Maynard brings his experience developing and leading high-growth companies. WIN provides its portfolio companies with mentorship and on-demand access to an affiliate network of more than eighty industry experts.

Webb is the chairman (and was formerly the CEO) of LiveOps, a cloud-based call center with a community of twenty thousand agents, and is a board member at both salesforce.com and Yahoo! Previously, he was the COO of eBay, where he created organizational processes and day-to-day structures that enabled eBay to grow from $140 million in revenue to more than $6 billion in 2006. Webb has also served on several public and private boards, including Gartner (NYSE: IT), Niku (NASD: NIKU), Extensity (NASD: EXTN), Hyperion (NASD: HYSL),

Peribit (acquired by Juniper Networks), Baynote, and AdMob (acquired by Google), where he was also one of the first investors.

In 2004, Maynard and his wife created the Webb Family Foundation, which provides underprivileged, motivated young individuals access to quality education.

Webb lives in Silicon Valley with his wife, Irene. For more information, please visit www.rebootingwork.com.

Carlye Adler is an award-winning journalist and bestselling author. Her writing has been published in *Fast Company*, *Fortune*, *Forbes*, *Newsweek*, *Time*, and *Wired* and has been anthologized in *The Best Business Stories of the Year*. She is the coauthor of two books with salesforce.com chairman and CEO Marc Benioff: the national bestseller *Behind the Cloud* and *The Business of Changing the World*. She is also a coauthor with Jennifer Aaker and Andy Smith of *The Dragonfly Effect: Quick, Effective, and Powerful Ways to Use Social Media to Drive Social Change*. Her books have been translated into Chinese, Greek, Korean, Indonesian, Japanese, Russian, and Vietnamese. She lives in New York. For more information, please visit www.carlyeadler.com.

Index